MW01706428

DARE

TO SUCCEED

Warren Veenman & Sally Eichhorst

Reach Publishers
Kwa-Zulu Natal, South Africa

Also by Warren Veenman & Sally Eichhorst:

Unleash Your Full Potential

ISBN 0 620 25766 0

Published by Reach Publishers, P.O.Box, 1384, Wandsbeck, South Africa, 3631
Printed and bound by Pinetown Printers(Pty) Ltd, 16 Ivy Road, Pinetown, 3600
Edited by Janine Williams and Sian Chaplin
Cover designed by Reach Publishers

Contents

This book is dedicated to the remarkable beauty, talent and potential every one of us has inside. The object of this book is to make you see it and dare to unleash it.

Dare to succeed

Dare to spread your wings and fly.
Dare to love with all your might.
Dare to stand out amongst the crowd.
Dare to live the life you truly want.

Dare to make a stand for what you believe.
Dare to face a challenge.
Dare to dream and make it real.

In a nutshell: DARE TO SUCCEED!

Sally Eichhorst

Introduction

Don't be afraid your life will end;
be afraid that it will never begin.
Grace Hansen

Success is a word that means so many different things to people. For you it may mean making more money, or finding more happiness, love or fame. We don't know what your definition of success is. What we do know is that whatever your present circumstances, you can achieve the success you desire. There is nothing in the world stopping you from achieving success, but yourself.

The reason why most people don't succeed in life is because they either **don't believe they can** or **because they simply don't know how**. The fact is that we all already have the potential within us to succeed, whether we believe it or not. We're born with it! Every single one of us has what it takes to reach our goals and achieve success and happiness. This is what our book is all about. It is a basic, understandable, practical and easy to read book that will show you how you can reach the success you desire.

We believe, without a shadow of a doubt that if you follow the practical principles and ideas outlined in this book, you will achieve and live the life of your dreams no matter what your present circumstances.

Whilst reading this book, we strongly recommend that you do the following:

- Read each chapter carefully, highlighting sections that make an impact on you.

- Once you have completed the book, go back and review these highlighted sections.

- Once read, this book should be kept close at hand and referred to often, to keep you motivated and moving in the right direction.

- Don't rush through these pages. Think about what you are reading and apply what you learn along the way. Only then will this book be of benefit to you.

People who say it cannot be done
should not interrupt those who are doing it.

Dennis Waitley

How often have you left a book unfinished? Did you know that statistics state that up to ninety percent of people who read a book do not finish it? Even more shocking is that they do not reach the second chapter. Is it any wonder that many of these people don't succeed in life? They lack the drive and effort so necessary for them to reach their dreams.

We urge you not to fall into this percentage and rather to read on and enjoy this time with us. The seconds, minutes and hours spent on this book will change your life.

By simply reading this book you are taking the first step towards achieving your ultimate life. Applying the principles in the following pages will ensure that you get there.

Come on and join us in this adventure of discovery and growth. We'll walk you through it. We assure you, when you reach the last pages, you will have all the tools necessary to SUCCEED IN LIFE.

Some make it happen, some watch it happen, and some say,
"What happened?"

Unknown

So be the one to make it happen…

Chapter 1

What is Stopping You?

The best place to find a helping hand
is at the end of your own arm.

Unknown

We strongly believe that most people are their own worst enemies when it comes to their reasons for not succeeding. In this chapter please bear with us as we state the harsh facts as we see them.

Today is the age of the W.W.W. and we don't mean the World Wide Web. We mean it's the age of the Whingers, Whiners and Wishful thinkers!

You're either one of them or you know tons of them. This breed of people seem to have multiplied over the years, growing into a depressing swamp of negativity, pulling many down with them. It's quite correctly said that to push someone off the edge into a negative swamp is far easier than pulling them up out of a negative swamp. As a result, many have joined the masses in a whining and whinging chorus of destruction.

You probably think we're being a little harsh, but the fact of the matter is that whinging, whining and wishful thinking never got anyone anywhere, no matter what their circumstances.

Why does it get them nowhere? Because the whingers, whiners and wishful thinkers DO NOTHING about their grievances! They're often experts when it comes to moaning and groaning, but useless at doing anything about it. They're masters at offering excuses for their failures and lack of success and their true talent often lies in blaming others or outside forces for everything that goes wrong.

Does this sound like you? If so, be assured you're going nowhere fast! It's like anything in life. We can debate, talk, whine, moan, screech and squeal until we're blue in the face, but it doesn't get us anywhere. It's taking action by giving ourselves a good old kick in the butt that makes things happen.

We have friends, relatives and associates who are constantly complaining about their jobs. They whine endlessly about how bored they are, how unfair the boss is, how they have no growth opportunities, how they are underpaid and overworked.

Then the same people or others whine ceaselessly about their relationships. They repeat again and again the same sob story about how they are bored, taken for granted, never see that person enough, the other isn't romantic or affectionate enough.

Of course the list of complaints that are up there on the number one position of popularity and overuse are those that involve the times that we are living in. One of the most common reasons why people don't succeed in life is that they blame their failures on the times that they are living in. They adopt a totally pessimistic outlook regarding their country and the world as a whole.

The thing is, every generation seems to think they have it bad. People have been complaining about the same sort of issues since the year dot. The whingers have just grown in number, that's all!

So what do we say to all the whiners, whingers and wishful thinkers? It doesn't matter what they're complaining about; whether it's the job, relationship, physical appearance or hard times, our response is the same. **'SO WHAT ARE YOU DOING ABOUT IT?'**

This question literally stops them in their tracks because it's the last thing they expect or want to hear. You see they expect you to join them in their whinging and whining, agree with them and sympathize with them. They certainly don't want to hear you ask the unthinkable, **'WHAT ARE YOU DOING ABOUT IT?'** This is because they usually don't plan to do anything about it. It's usually too much work, effort, responsibility or willpower to do anything. By asking them this question, you have now cornered them into facing the uncomfortable reality that they have no plan, intention or energy to really do anything about it.

Leonard was your typical W.W.W. (Whiner, Whinger and Wishful Thinker). That was until he decided to do something about his situation.

Today, Leonard is a successful attorney who owns his own practice. What makes Leonard so unique? Well 12 years ago, this same man was a sales rep, working on a commission basis only. He wanted much more out of life, but due to his poor background and other complications, he never even finished high school. Opportunities were scarce for someone with no qualifications. ‘I was even 40 kilograms overweight at that stage,’ he told us as he fondly patted his flat belly.

What happened? What made a man change everything so drastically? Let him tell you how and why!

‘I woke up one morning, feeling the worst I had ever felt in my life. Not only did I have a killer of a hangover, but both my eyes and lips were swollen from a punch up the night before. As usual it was my fault. I was drunk and out of control again. All I could vaguely remember was a nice girl and then her giant boyfriend's fist.

How I hated myself that morning! I hated my job! I hated the way I lived! I hated being fat! I was tired of being lonely. If I had a gun, I probably would have ended my misery then and there. That’s how low I felt.

I remember shouting at the top of my voice, "Enough! Enough!"

I screamed these words over and over again. I was tired of envying others. I had more than I could stand of this loser that was me.

I didn’t go to work that day, but went down to the beach alone. (Alone, now that was a word I could relate to) There I sat with a piece of paper and a pen and wrote down what I really wanted from life.

I didn’t bother about how I was going to get these things. I just wrote down what I wanted more than anything else in the world. Things that would make me the happiest person alive!

Well, at the time, if anyone had seen my list, they would have thought I was crazier than ever. I wanted to have a great body. I wanted to be an attorney. I wanted to have my own office with my name on the door. I wanted to have someone to love. I wanted to be wealthy. I wanted to have real friends. Indeed, I wanted a lot!

You know, I have achieved every single one of those things I wrote on that list. How? Well first I stopped whinging and whining about my situation and started doing something about it. I also replaced wishful thinking with action.

From that second, I promised myself that nothing would stop me from living the life I truly wanted and I would give my all to get there.

To help me stay on track, I read books about other people who had achieved their goals with all the odds seemingly stacked against them.

The person that gave me the most inspiration was Helen Keller. Here was a woman who was blind and deaf and still became a successful author and lecturer, dedicating her life to help others believe in themselves and achieve great things. I thought if she could do it, I have no excuses.

I pasted these words by Helen Keller on my bathroom mirror so that I saw it every day: **"I fall, I stand still… I trudge on, I gain a little… I get more eager and climb higher and begin to see the widening horizon. Every struggle is a victory."**

So if Leonard can do it, what is stopping you?

Remember, there is absolutely nothing stopping you from succeeding in life but yourself. Our aim in this book is to show you **how you can succeed**.

For you to succeed in life, there are 5 important areas you must work on. Neglecting any one or more of these areas can seriously cripple your attempts at success.

This book is divided into these 5 important parts....

Part 1

Awaken The Power Within

Choices

I did not choose to be born.
I could not choose my parents.
I had no choice regarding when and where I was born.
I had no choice about how I was brought up.
But there comes a time when I must take responsibility for the choices I can make.
In the end, I can choose how I will live.

Sally Eichhorst

Chapter 2

The Power Of Thoughts

"Nothing can stop the man
with the right mental attitude from achieving his goal;
nothing can help the man with the wrong mental attitude."
Thomas Jefferson

We have known Alfred Jackson for many years. Alf is one of those rare breeds of people who has this wonderful talent called Optimism. He possesses this extraordinary gift to always see the bright side of any situation and we have yet to see him in a foul and gloomy mood or without a smile on his dial.

Alf has this natural ability to spread cheer and encouragement to all he comes into contact with. His favourite words are, 'Smile awhile and give your face a rest!'

Alf owns a large jewellery store in a prime shopping area and has employed the same staff for the past ten years. Why have all these people faithfully remained with him? No, not because of the money, but due to his ATTITUDE! They all maintain that Alf has an unshakeable, positive attitude and he somehow spreads it to them by motivating, inspiring, encouraging and generally helping them to see that there are positives to be found even in the worst situations. When Alf is around problems become manageable challenges. 'He's like a breath of fresh air!' said one of his doting staff members.

We asked Alf why he is always so positive and he replied, "I am positive and see the brighter side of life, not because I was fortunate enough to be born like this, but because I choose to be. I believe that we can all control our thoughts and what we choose to think about affects who we are and what we are capable of achieving. So I choose to live my life smiling and not frowning, laughing and not crying, singing and not shouting and most importantly, thinking positively and not negatively. Focusing on negatives never did anyone an ounce of good, but focusing on positives certainly does everyone the world of good!' Alf's parting advice to us was 'Smile awhile and give your face a rest!'

Approximately one year after this last chat with Alf, we heard that he had been hijacked at gunpoint, brutally assaulted, shot in the back and left for dead.

We went to see Alf in hospital and were greeted by his old familiar smiling face and the laughter of nurses around him. He told us that he had nearly died but thanks to the medical staff working around the clock to keep their promise, he eventually pulled through. 'What promise?' We asked him. 'Well,' Alf answered, 'While I was on the operating table and barely conscious I noticed that everyone around me wore deep frowns of concern and worry, making it obvious that they believed me to be on my way out.'

'Before going under, I mustered up all my strength and said as loud as possible, "Wait, I'm allergic to something!" The medical team all froze in their tracks and everyone's attention was momentarily focused on my next words. "I'm allergic to death!" I said. This statement was followed by a roar of laughter from the medical team who seemed to relax a little. Whilst I still had the energy to speak, I asked them to promise me one thing. " Promise me that you will treat me like a new life coming into the world and not like an old life, leaving the world. Birth is a happy, positive thing, so focus on that when you work on me. Now smile awhile and give your face a rest!'

How did this experience affect Alf'? When we asked him he said, 'You know I'm very lucky, as that bullet just missed my spine and I could have been left paralysed. My wife thinks the scars are sexy and to top it off, now I'm even more determined to live life to the full.'

Unlike Alf, who sees the positive in any situation, most people seem to focus on the negatives. They focus on their weaknesses, rather than their strengths and often blame everyone and everything but themselves for their circumstances and failures in life.

They blame their parents, their upbringing, their education, their financial situation. They even blame their country, the economy, the crime and the times they're living in.

Two men went to the Australian outback
to sell shoes for their Shoe Company.
One called his boss and said.
"Sir, there's no opportunity here, no one wears shoes.
The second man, called his boss and exclaimed
"Sir, there's tremendous opportunity here, no one wears shoes!"
Unknown

It's a matter of choice whether you look for blame externally for your failures or you try and find potential opportunities in difficult situations. As Winston Churchill said, 'The pessimist sees difficulty in every opportunity. The optimist sees opportunity in every difficulty.'

The main reason why most people never achieve what they want from life is that they are too busy looking for scapegoats to blame for their lack of success. These people fill their minds with pessimistic and negative thoughts, leaving little space for anything else. In other words, they are preventing their minds from discovering their true capabilities, as there is no room for the right positive thoughts.

If you continually think about all the reasons why you will never succeed in life, you are creating a person who has all the reasons in the world not to succeed and is sure to fail.

The key to achieving what you want from life lies in your ability to choose the right positive thoughts. You simply cannot allow yourself to underestimate the importance of what you think. What you think is what you are! It is a fact that your daily thoughts eventually influence the person you become.

You live with your thoughts, so be careful what they are.
Unknown

If it's in our best interests to consistently think positively, why don't most of us do so all day, every day? The answer lies in our common weakness of exposing our minds to negative influences.

This negative influence takes root from an early age. As a

child, everything in life looks positive. We feel we can conquer the world, achieve the impossible, embark on adventures, believe wholeheartedly in ourselves, feel we can be and do anything we desire - that is until we are told otherwise, forever influencing our thoughts and beliefs.

Irrespective of who we are, we are all born with a clean and positive slate that is our minds. At this stage we are unaware of what is right or wrong, good or evil and what we can or cannot do. However, with time, like a sponge, our minds absorb influences from everything and everyone around us.

So take care and be aware of what you allow to influence your mind, as your ability to succeed in everything you do, relies on you creating a mind dominated by positive thoughts.

Forget 'I can't' for those are the words of a coward and failure.
Remember 'I'll try' for those are the words of a potential winner.
Respect and imitate 'I will' for those are the words of a winner.
Unknown

It is a mind dominated by Positive Thoughts that makes it possible for men to reach the pinnacle of their dreams and it is a mind dominated by Negative Thoughts that keeps others wallowing at the bottom, never rising and amounting to anything.

When your mind is dominated with negative thoughts of hate, jealousy, worry and envy, how can you hope to maximise your potential and achieve anything? However, when your mind is dominated with positive thoughts of love, sincerity, optimism, faith, courage, generosity, hope, ambition, confidence and initiative, you are maximising your potential and can achieve almost anything you set your mind to.

Those who soar amongst the winners are masters when it comes to tapping into that part of their mind, which promotes all their positive and empowering qualities.

How do you develop a mind that is dominated by positive thoughts? It is simply a case of always being aware and taking control of what thoughts you are feeding your mind. Whenever a negative thought tries to creep in, you must force it out and replace it with a positive thought. It's certainly not as easy as it sounds, especially if you have a lot of problems and worries, but with practice it eventually becomes a habit to think positively.

If you are determined to focus your thoughts repetitively on the bad things in life, painting a picture of future doom and gloom in your mind, then be prepared to fulfil your own negative forecast with frightening and hair-raising accuracy. If instead, you paint an optimistic picture of hope, courage and all the good things in life, then expect to attract these things to you.

" If you look at what you have in life,
You'll always have more.
If you look at what you don't have in life,
You'll never have enough."

Oprah Winfrey

Your mind can be likened to a garden and you are the gardener. You have two choices: you can either look after your garden or you can ignore it. Whatever you do, one thing is certain, your garden will grow, whether you decide to look after it or not. However to reap the rewards of a beautiful and well kept garden you must be prepared to put in the necessary effort. So make the effort every day to feed your mind with positive thoughts and protect it from negative thoughts and you will reap unimaginable rewards.

Sally's positive game plan

A prime example of why we should try and take control of our thoughts, especially those about ourselves, takes place on the squash court. What's squash got to do with it, you wonder? Well, see if this sounds at all familiar?

I enjoy a regular game of social squash to thrash out any excess energy or occasional stress I may have. The leading man in this story is one of my squash partners who will remain anonymous, to spare his dignity and masculinity. We'll call him 'Rambo.'

The thing is, I'm certain that he is actually a better player than I am, but things fall apart when 'Rambo' makes a mistake. He starts up an abusive conversation with himself, which becomes progressively worse as further mistakes are made. 'Stupid, stupid idiot. That was absolutely pathetic. Monkeys play better. I can't play to save my life. Clumsy fool!'

Obviously I cannot repeat some of the insults he hurls at himself through gritted teeth as he storms around the court like an angry, stampeding bull, nostrils flaring and literally steaming with self-hatred and disgust. Of course, I encourage him by saying things like, ' Losing against a little woman!'

The end result is always the same. I win and 'Rambo' wonders where he went wrong.

So many people are either like my friend 'Rambo' or know dozens of people like him who constantly speak negatively about themselves, insulting, criticizing and putting themselves down repetitively.

There will be those of you who just cannot believe that anything you say or think repeatedly can have any effect on you. You could not be more mistaken!

By repeating thoughts or statements, day in and day out, you eventually convince your subconscious that these thoughts or statements are true. These thoughts or statements then become deep-rooted beliefs and your subconscious will find ways to make them a reality, even against your better judgement.

'Rambo' will never win until he changes the way he repeatedly communicates with himself.

"It doesn't matter what anyone thinks or says about you. What really matters is what you think and say about yourself!"

Unknown

Becoming a master at communicating with yourself

What others say to you or think of you has little affect on your well-being, when compared to the opinion you have of yourself and what you say to yourself.

To become a master at communicating with yourself, you can start by making a pact of your own, that from this moment on, you will stop criticising and judging yourself too harshly. There are enough people out in the world who will criticise and judge you, so give yourself a break and don't add to it.

Remember, that mentally repeating to yourself, ‘stupid fool,’ or ‘I can’t do it,’ or feeding your mind with words like worthless, ugly, stupid, dumb, eventually becomes a belief in your subconscious and you will start becoming like this.

From now on, when you talk to yourself, use words like ‘I can do it, I’m the best’ and watch the positive change that comes over all your actions.

Be selective of what you say over and over to yourself, making sure that it builds you up rather than puts you down.

The minute you start talking about what you’re going to do if you lose, you have lost.

George Shultz

Chapter 3

The Power Of Belief

" It's a funny thing about life;
If you refuse to accept anything but the best,
You very often get it."

Somerset Maugham

During a motivational seminar we presented for National Women's Day, a young lady suddenly sat up to attention as we spoke about the incredible power of belief. She then enthusiastically shared the following amazing story with us.

A good friend of hers was waiting impatiently at home for her husband and growing angrier by the second. He had promised he would come straight home from work, but was once more extremely late and was obviously having drinks somewhere.

When her husband finally arrived, he walked in through the back door via the kitchen to avoid his wife, as he knew she would be very angry with him. He was feeling a little tired from the drinks he'd had with the guys after work and headed for the bedroom to have a quick nap. On his way through the kitchen, amongst other things, he noticed a pot of water on the stove. Without giving it a second thought, he then sneaked into the bedroom and lay his weary body down.

The next thing he remembered was his wife's angry voice shouting his name and waking him from a deep sleep. He opened his eyes to the sight of his wife standing over him with a pot in her hands. A quick flash of memory came into focus - the same pot on the stove in the kitchen - boiling water! It dawned on him that she was going to throw the boiling water over him. Terror-stricken and in mid-screech he looked on as she did indeed throw the pot of water over him. He yelled in pain as his skin instantly became scorched and blistered.

What's so amazing about this story? Well, the pot of water the wife actually threw over her husband was only cold tap water! However, he believed without a doubt that it was the same pot he had seen on the stove earlier with boiling water in it. Because he believed so emphatically that it was boiling water, when the cold water hit him, his mind and body reacted as though it was boiling water causing pain as well as scorches and blisters to occur on his skin. The brain simply does what it is told, acting upon what it believes to be true. The power and strength of one's will and belief cannot be underestimated. It is a massive force when handled correctly.

Beliefs hold incredible power, sometimes defying logic. There are numerous incidents whereby people achieved the 'impossible' only because they believed they could. Beliefs have even claimed the power to heal both mentally and physically, thereby baffling the medical profession.

We can all keep going long after we believe we can't.

Warren & Sally

During our research we were amazed to read about a case in America involving a Diabetic man with a split personality. When his personality changed from one character to another, so did the colour of his eyes. Even more amazing, was the fact that the second personality had no trace of Diabetes. This was because he so emphatically believed that he had two separate personalities.

This is the amazing power of belief!

One of the most important ingredients to success is a strong belief in yourself and your capabilities. Those who succeed have an uplifting, confident and positive belief in themselves. They believe that they will succeed. Those who fail, have a poor image of themselves, believing before they've even begun that they will fail.

However, merely hoping or wishing for something is a useless exercise. You must believe that it can and will be yours. If you believe strongly enough in yourself and your capabilities, you can do almost anything you set your mind to.

I hoped and wished and received nothing.
I imagined and believed and received everything.

Warren & Sally

Beliefs According To Fleas

Ever wondered how Flea Trainers stop the fleas from escaping their enclosure? Well, it's a simple theory of belief that works every time.

The fleas are put in a box with the lid on. The fleas repeatedly try to jump out of the box, but are unable to as the lid prevents their escape. After some time when the lid is eventually removed, the fleas continue to jump, but they will not jump high enough to escape the box. Why not? Because they believe they can't!

Of course they can, but by repeatedly trying unsuccessfully with the lid on, they eventually resign themselves to the fact that it's impossible, with the result that it literally becomes impossible even with the lid off. They have conditioned themselves to jump only so high and that is all they believe they can do.

In the same respect, if you have limiting beliefs about yourself, you are restricted from creating the life you want and achieving all you are capable of.

Don't let yourself or others limit you by putting a lid on your potential. If you wish to reach your full potential, you have to rid yourself of the limiting beliefs, which hold you back. Start believing that you can do anything that you put your mind to. If you allow others to put limits on you or if you limit yourself, you will eventually start to believe that you have these limits and behave accordingly.

You have to ask yourself, 'What limiting beliefs have I inherited?' Then work on getting rid of them and replacing them with uplifting and positive beliefs.

Here are just a few examples of some people's ridiculously limiting beliefs....

"You'd better learn secretarial skills or else get married."
Modelling agency, rejecting Marilyn Monroe in 1944

"Can't act. Can't sing. Slightly bald. Can dance a little."
A film company's verdict on Fred Astaire's 1928 screen test

"Everything that can be invented has been invented."
Director of the US Patent Office, 1899

"The aeroplane is scientifically impossible."
Royal Society president Lord Kelvin, 1897-9

"Brain work will cause women to go bald."
Berlin professor, 1914

"We don't like their sound, and guitar music is on the way out."
Decca Recording Co. rejecting the Beatles, 1962

What you believe is what you get!

If you believe that you cannot succeed because there are no opportunities out there for you, you are absolutely correct. The only reason you see no possibilities is because you have conditioned yourself to believe just that. Indeed, you will never reap the benefits of all the opportunities out there, until you believe that these prospects exist for you.

Whenever you doubt this, think of people who have yet to be born, who will eventually grab at the very opportunities you missed, rising to the top of their professions, running their own successful companies and enjoying great wealth. Amongst them will also be those who are going to become the great leaders of tomorrow, Presidents of their nations and athletic heroes. We believe that you have an advantage over them as you are alive now and they have yet to be born. Stop making excuses!

If you believe that you will fail, you will! If you believe that you will succeed, you will! If you believe you will be rich, you will be rich. If you believe you are destined for poverty, you will never rise above that. Those who achieve success in any form, value themselves highly. They choose to think rich thoughts and therefore receive the wealth that life has to offer. **Remember that the bridge that leads to riches is built on rich thinking.**

Believing that your business, your happiness, your health or your success in life is impossible, is the best way to make it so.
Warren & Sally

How to develop belief in yourself

There is only one way to develop a powerful, positive and uplifting belief in yourself and that is to think only powerful, positive and uplifting thoughts. Remember, *'Sooner or later the man that wins is the man that thinks he can.'*

Imagine that an opportunity arises for you to go into your own business. What do you think your chances of success would be if your thoughts and beliefs were, 'I could be making a mistake. I may not make it on my own. I won't have any security. I always fail. The economy is bad?' Would you be confident, excited and motivated? Not likely! You would be going into it half-heartedly, because your mind would be dominated by negative beliefs. Your chances of succeeding would be minimal.

However, what would your chances of succeeding be, if your thoughts and beliefs were, 'I will make it work. I can do it. I will succeed no matter what?' Exceptionally good, as you have instructed your brain that you expect to succeed. You now act with excitement, motivation and confidence, tapping into your hidden potential. Just as failure feeds upon failure, success breeds success. The sky is now the limit!

We urge you to start now by believing that you are capable of the success you so deserve from life. Your beliefs hold great power. Exercise them now.

During one of our motivational workshops we chatted to a gentleman who had once been a teacher. He told us an interesting story about one of the young boys he had taught. This particular boy had a below average I.Q. and should actually have been in one of the lower streams. Yet, he was in the 'A' stream and always came amongst the top ten in class. How was this possible? Because no one had told the boy any different. He didn't know that he had a below average I.Q. and therefore he did not think and believe that his chances of being placed in the top ten of the schools highest achievers was unlikely. Because he had achieved good grades through hard work before, he believed he could do so again and indeed he stunned staff members by achieving well over his estimated potential time and time again.

If you believe 'I can,' you are correct. If you believe, 'I can't,' you are also completely correct. It is a fact that you become like the person you think and believe you are and achieve only what you think and believe you are capable of. Although this is a bold statement, it is absolutely true.

What you think about repetitively has a major effect on your current situation. Why would thinking about something repetitively have such a major effect on your life and the situation you find yourself in today?

Well, when you paint a clear picture in your mind of what you can or cannot do, you better equip your brain to make it become a reality. If you really think about something, seeing it as clear as day in your mind and bringing back this thought again and again, your brain will eventually begin to believe it is really true. This belief results in all your actions being geared towards transforming that thought into reality.

If you presently find yourself very unhappy with your situation, you need to look at what you are thinking about all day long. If you are constantly thinking about everything that has gone wrong, is going wrong and could still go wrong in your life, then you are guaranteed not to rise above your present situation.

What you must do no matter what your present situation, is to constantly force yourself to rather focus your thoughts on what you want from life and where you want to be in life. Focusing on these positives is the only way you will ever rise above your present situation.

You alone have the power to choose what you think about all day long. You have total control of this one thing, your thoughts. By repeating the right positive thoughts you are ultimately able to influence your beliefs and therefore your life for the better.

Never underestimate the power of your thoughts and your beliefs!

Part 2

Attitude And Understanding Determines Success

People are like stained-glass windows.
They sparkle and shine when the sun is out,
but when the darkness sets in,
their true beauty is revealed only if there is a light from within.
Elizabeth Kübler-Ross

Chapter 4

Why Adjust your Attitude and Understanding?

*"If there is any one secret of success,
it lies in the ability to get the other person's point of view and see
things from that person's angle as well as from your own"*
Henry Ford

It is a fact that most of the problems throughout the world, whether between countries, cultures, companies, employees, family or friends can often be traced back to a misunderstanding between people or a lack of understanding between them.

Those who have a good understanding of others will always have a far greater chance of success. Why? Because a genuine understanding of others, leads to a better understanding of oneself. This helps us to adjust our attitude in dealing with others, drawing people to us and creating all sorts of opportunities. In this way we can get what we want more easily from others; we can generally perform better in all that we do and we can avoid conflict born from misunderstandings.

Therefore we should all strive to work on our ability to get along with people by understanding and caring about their emotions. In other words we should learn to have more empathy for people in general.

To succeed in any area of our lives we have to broaden our understanding of others as well as be prepared to change our attitude. To do this, there are 5 important areas we need to work on.

The following 5 chapters will show you how to adjust your attitude and have a better understanding of others. Working on these 5 areas will not only make you a better person but will change every aspect of your life for the better….

Chapter 5

Exercise Self-control

(Area 1)

" For every sixty seconds of anger or envy,
You lose an entire minute of happiness."

Warren & Sally

Put your brain in gear before you put your thoughts in motion - ENVY

An important aspect of self-control is envy. Let Sue Anne explain the poison of envy!

I'm a volunteer 'companion' at a frail care hospital and spend an hour a week visiting those in need of a little friendship and companionship. That night I had chosen to visit with Mrs. Aylesbury.

'Let me tell you about the poison of envy,' Mrs. Aylesbury said as I sat at her bedside. It was the first time I had visited her and I was told that she had taken a turn for the worse since her old roommate had passed away.

Mrs. Aylesbury gazed longingly at the empty bed beside hers and a large tear rolled slowly down her cheek. 'I miss Mrs. Darby so much,' she whispered. 'She and I not only shared this room for a long time, but we also shared our lives, our loves, our experiences and so many of our dreams during all our hours of chatting. Oh I was so happy then,' she croaked as she battled to choke back another tear.

'You see, Mrs. Darby and I were both bedridden, but she was still able to sit up whilst it is best for me to remain flat on my back as sitting up is very painful. She occupied the bed next to the window and because I could not sit up she would look out of that window and describe what she saw for me. She described a lovely park, full of colourful flowers and large trees. There was a lake with ducks and swans and all sorts of other lovely birds, which would come and go. She would excitedly describe them all to me in great detail,' said Mrs. Aylesbury with a sad smile.

'She would tell me about the people having picnics under the shade of the trees, the lovers walking hand in hand through the park and the mothers walking their prams. It seemed like there was always something interesting happening on the other side of that window and Mrs. Darby described every detail to me so that it would be as real for me as possible and so I could also experience it all through my imagination. Those were the best of times. I lived for her stories of what she saw through that window as it somehow made me feel connected again to the outside world.

I'm not sure exactly when it changed, but it started as a nagging little thought and grew into an ugly boil of envy. One day whilst Mrs. Darby was describing the lovely swan she called Emma, gracefully swimming through the lake, I suddenly thought, "It's not fair! I want to see it for myself . I want to be in Mrs. Darby's bed by the window and be able to experience all those wonderful things first hand. Why should she get to have all the fun?"

It was just a thought at first, but one thought led to another and then it got stronger, growing and brooding within me until it became an ugly and obsessive envy, which seemed to have taken over my mind. I became truly obsessed with wanting what Mrs. Darby had. Obsessed with being in Mrs. Darby's shoes and being able to see all the wonderful sights through the window.

I was awoken late one night by Mrs. Darby's coughing. She seemed to be choking and battling to breathe. I just lay there watching her when instead I should have rung the panic button to alert the night nurse. It's all my fault! Why didn't I press that button? I remember just lying there and listening to her until there was nothing more to listen to - not even breathing!

Later the next day they removed Mrs. Darby and the bed by the window lay empty. Of course I asked to be moved there as soon as was appropriate, for I was fixated on that window and the pleasure its sights could bring me during my last days.

As soon as I was alone I managed to lift myself painfully and very slowly to a sitting position and strained to look out of the window. It faced only a blank brick wall. Mrs. Darby was making up the scenery for me. Do you understand - she knew how much I enjoyed and lived for her stories. She was doing it all for me!'

Now Mrs. Aylesbury was crying hysterically as I sat white-faced and shocked at her story.

The moral of the story is that envy only causes unnecessary pain, grief and resentment. Don't be too quick to envy another as you may not know the full story! So always **'Put your brain in gear before you put your thoughts in motion.'**

Think more about what you can get rather than what you can give and your life may take a turn for the worse.

Warren & Sally

Put your brain in gear before you put your mouth in motion - ANGER

Joey was a twelve year old boy with a very bad temper, which often got him into trouble. His parents had pondered often about how to rid their son of this bad character trait. They were at a loss until Joey's grandfather came to stay. Grandpa Max was a wise old man who decided to take the matter of Joey's anger in hand. He sat Joey down and they had a long chat. He said a lot of interesting things, and explained to Joey that unless he controlled his anger, he would always be sure to lose out in life.

After speaking to Grandpa Max, Joey wanted to get rid of his anger but still found it hard to control. Grandpa Max decided to help him by making him agree to the following experiment.

In their backyard, they had a big white wall on which was erected a basketball hoop for Joey to practice shots and play with his friends. Grandpa Max told Joey that every time he lost his temper, he had to chip out a little piece of the wall with a chisel and keep all the chipped out pieces together in a pile in front of the wall.

On the first day Joey had chipped a grand total of thirty pieces out of the wall and they lay in a destructive heap in front of the wall. As the days passed, this number slowly shrank. Joey found that it took more effort to chisel chips out of the wall than it did to avoid losing his temper. He also found that the wall looked ugly and damaged and he preferred it as it had been.

Finally, there came a day when Joey didn't lose his temper even once. He proudly announced this to Grandpa Max, who told him that for every day he was able to avoid resorting to anger, he should pick a piece from the pile at the foot of the wall and fill one of the chips with it.

Many days later, Joey was eventually able to show his Grandpa that all the chips were filled. Together they stood, hand in hand in front of the wall. Grandpa Max told Joey that he was proud of him, but although he had done a great job, the wall did not look the same. Joey had tried to fill the chips as best he could, but little cracks and small holes were still visible. It would take a lot of work to repair the wall properly and restore it to its good old self.

Grandpa Max told Joey that every time he loses his temper and says something in anger or physically hurts someone in anger, he is leaving a wound or scar that may never heal, just like the remaining cracks and holes in the wall. Sometimes no amount of 'sorries' can heal someone you've hurt with your anger, just as numerous attempts at painstakingly filling in the chips that you made may never restore the wall to its original self.

This was a lesson that Joey never forgot and always made him think twice before resorting to anger. Whenever he felt himself becoming angry he remembered the following words of his Grandpa Max, 'The winds of anger will always blow out the lamp of intelligence.'

Speak when you're angry,
and you'll make the best speech you'll ever regret.

Lawrence J. Peter

Next time you open your mouth to say something hurtful, remember that you may leave a wound or scar that may never heal. The damage is done and is often very difficult to undo. So always **'Put your brain in gear before you put your mouth in motion.'** All it takes is a little bit of self-control!

Chapter 6

Stop Judging

(Area2)

Never look down on anybody unless you're helping him up.
The Reverend Jesse Jackson

We were in the pet shop the other day picking up some odds and ends for our five spoilt Jack Russell puppies. Whilst browsing, we happened to overhear a heated conversation between the storeowner and another man.

The storeowner was negotiating with a man selling him a litter of puppies. They seemed to be disagreeing about something and as we got closer we heard the storeowner say, 'I definitely don't want that one. I'll take the other five for the agreed price, but the one that's not normal goes.'

The man replied, 'But it's only a scar and it's barely noticeable. Anyway it happened over a month ago and the vet says he's fine.'

'I don't care what the vet says,' scoffed the storeowner. 'He's damaged goods, scarred for life. I know I will battle to get rid of him because no one wants a puppy who is already scarred,' the storeowner half-shouted.

At first we hadn't noticed the woman and the boy who were in the store with us. Evidently, they had seen and heard what we had and now approached the storeowner and the other man. The woman seemed strangely angry and irritable. Her anger was directed at the storeowner and we were afraid she might wrestle him to the ground and beat him to a pulp.

'No one is ever scarred for life. It is people like you who label them as damaged goods and see them as abnormal that scar them for life!' she said angrily to the storeowner.

We looked at each other in silent agreement. This woman was definitely overreacting! We couldn't believe that she was losing her temper over something that clearly was none of her business. Our first impression was, 'What an angry and rude woman!'

'Let me see that puppy,' demanded the angry woman. The man held out the puppy in question and the boy with her giggled delightedly. He immediately grabbed the puppy and hugged it close.

'Look mom, he has a big scar just like mine. Can I keep him? My friends at school say I don't look so good myself and the puppy will understand because he's just like me,' said the boy as he looked lovingly into the puppy's eyes.

Just then we saw the boy clearly for the first time. His face was terribly disfigured and a number of deep scars were visible even from a distance.

'I'd like to buy the puppy,' the woman said to both men.

Both men looked terribly uncomfortable and embarrassed and the storeowner sheepishly said, 'You can have him for free.'

The woman became even angrier as she replied, ‘I said I’d like to buy the puppy. Just because it is scarred, does not mean that it is worthless. This puppy is worth just as much as all the others, if not more. I’ll pay the full price, thank you.’ And off she went with her son carrying one happy and soon to be spoilt rotten puppy.

That day we learnt a valuable lesson that we will never forget. 'Never judge anyone until you have walked in their shoes.' We had made the mistake of pre-judging this woman before we knew the full story. Yes, she may have come across angry and rude, but she had reason to be. She was feeling emotional and frustrated because people probably labelled her son as abnormal due to his disfiguring scars. She was only being protective of her son. Looking through her eyes, we would have reacted the same.

A little understanding goes a long way - by Warren

I was the owner of a busy Health Centre catering for people from all walks of life. One day I got an urgent call from my receptionist downstairs asking me to come down immediately as there was an extremely rude person enquiring about joining the Health Centre.

What greeted me as I approached the reception area was a weather beaten old man with a mop of long thinning grey hair and the angriest face I had ever seen.
"What is wrong with this place?" he bellowed at the top of his voice. His wife grabbed his arm to try and pacify him, but to no avail. "All I want to know is why I should pay extra if I join

and want someone to supervise me all the time?" he shouted, whilst his face grew redder by the second. I was afraid his head might explode.

I hastily ushered them into my office so that he wouldn’t disturb the other members. It was the longest 100 metres I had ever walked, with him cursing and pointing a knotty finger at every person he came across telling them what he thought of this Club. In the distance I could see my receptionist rolling her eyes back and I knew how she felt.

I finally got them into my office, shut the door and managed to get them to sit down. I politely offered them something to drink, which was of course flatly refused.

Sitting there opposite this bitter and angry old man and his embarrassed wife, I wondered how anyone could tolerate this rude person.

"You have to understand that if we had to have someone monitoring every one of our members all the time, we would need hundreds of staff. As we sometimes have over 300 members training at any given time, this is impossible," I tried to explain to him. "But you could hire a personal trainer to monitor you, however this will cost you slightly more than the normal fee."

Before he could take off at me again, I hastily added, "But that policy doesn’t have to be, if you could explain to me why you need to be monitored all the time?"

"Typical," he bellowed angrily. "You just don’t care. My boy is stuck in a wheelchair for life because of some stupid car accident. He can also barely talk or use his right arm. It's obvious to me that you don't want his type around here. You just don't understand," he finished off emotionally.

"You're right, I can't understand how you must feel," I said quietly. "But one of my best friends Gary trains here at the gym. He was involved in a motor bike accident and lost both his arms. You know he's been looking for a suitable training partner for a long time now and your son seems just perfect."

When I sold the gym 5 years later, they were both still training 3 times a week. Gary has 2 artificial arms and his training partner was walking with the aid of a walking stick. His father and mother also joined and became regular users of the gym and good friends of mine.

The next time you have the opportunity to judge someone, think twice before you judge them too quickly and too harshly. Remember, if you had lived their lives, experienced their problems, had their family and friends and were faced with all that life had thrown at them, chances are that you would behave exactly like them. A little understanding in these circumstances goes a long way!

Chapter 7

Be Kind, Helpful And Uplifting To All You Meet

(Area 3)

One of the most difficult things to give away is kindness.
It is usually returned.

Unknown

If people in general are never kind, helpful and uplifting to you, then why even bother to be kind, helpful and uplifting to all you meet?

Simply because it is a proven fact that if you are kind, helpful and uplifting to all those you come into contact with, every aspect of your life is guaranteed to improve. You will rid yourself almost entirely of depression and worry. You will create an abundance of happiness by attracting new friends and receiving warmth and affection from all you meet. You will produce an aura around you that will attract riches and blessings from others. Amongst other things you will also create a tremendous boost for your physical and mental well-being.

It is one of the most beautiful compensations of this life that no man can sincerely try to help another without helping himself.

Ralph Waldo Emerson

This doesn't mean that you must be a Superhero fighting crime and saving lives or give everything you own to others and generally letting people take advantage of you. Sometimes it is just the small things in life that make all the difference, like a kind word, a friendly smile, a helping hand or a word of encouragement when it is really needed.

No act of kindness, no matter how small, is ever wasted.

Aesop

From this moment on, give a friendly greeting to all those you come in contact with regardless of their position in life. Whether it's the chap at the corner who polishes your shoes, the security guard at the door, the lift operator, your secretary, your spouse, your children or any other person you meet, give a smile, talk, listen, understand, care for and give a kind word to all these people.

In other words, offer kindness and encouragement to those clearly in need thereof. Compliment, praise and thank from the heart. Give, no matter how little to those in need. Join a voluntary charity group, where all you need give is a little of your time and effort. The list of ways to help others and put a smile on their faces is endless. Putting a smile on another's face has a way of automatically putting a smile on your own. So smile…. If you can't get the corners up, just let the middle sag. Remember also that a smile is the most cost-effective way to instantly improve your looks.

A smile is a curve that sets everything straight.
Phyllis Diller

Strangely, life has a way of returning your good deeds and sometime, somehow you will be blessed tenfold – "What goes around, comes around." So the more you give of yourself, the more you will get. Just as, "The more you share, the more you will receive."

If you do this you are sure to grow from strength to strength, removing all negative and depressing thoughts. If you keep to yourself and give nothing, you are bound to drown in your own worries, fears and depression.

Kindness is the oil that takes the friction out of life
Anonymous

'I changed one thing in my life and it changed everything for the better,' Jim Reever told us over lunch one day.

'Two years ago my life was a mess and I mean a complete mess!' he laughed.

'My wife and I hardly spoke to each other and she was even contemplating divorce. Business was bad and my staff were totally unreliable. You know, they used to call me "Jim Reever the Grim Reaper" behind my back. Even my friends stopped calling as I was always in a foul mood.

I knew I had to do something as my life was falling apart around me. There were days I just didn't want to get up,' he admitted.

'At first I doubted your advice as it sounded too simple. Surely the act of being genuinely kind, helpful and uplifting to all I meet could not turn my life around? But I had nothing to lose and decided to try it out starting the following morning.

The next morning I awoke and greeted my wife with a big smile and a kiss before I made off to the bathroom. The look on her face was a sight to behold. When I left for work I again kissed her goodbye. (You know we had stopped doing that a long time ago)

As I parked my car I greeted the parking attendant. I spoke to the guard at the door to our building asking him how he was. He mentioned his daughter was sick and I made a mental note to remember this as well as her name. I chatted to the people in the lift. These were people who had worked on the same floor as me for the past four years and yet this was the first time I had spoken to them. When I got into the office I greeted all my staff with a big cheery smile and called a general meeting. I told them that I was aware that they had nicknamed me 'Jim Reever the Grim Reaper' and their faces dropped. They thought I was probably going to fire the lot of them, but instead I said that they should continue to call me by that nickname until I could prove to them that I didn't deserve it anymore.'

Did applying this principle change Jim's life? You bet!
'When I got home that night, my wife had made us a romantic dinner. I can't go into that any further or I'll have you blushing' he chuckled. 'My marriage literally improved immediately and we are due for a second honeymoon soon.

Business has improved to such an extent that I have been able to expand tremendously. My staff are loyal and reliable and I was even invited to a staff member's wedding and asked to be the Master of Ceremonies.

I have made so many more good friends and contacts since I adopted this simple way of life. What a different world this would be if we all adopted this simple philosophy!'

You make a living by what you get,
but you make a life by what you give.
Winston Churchill

The power of upliftment

We all need to be appreciated. No matter who we are or what we do, we need to feel that we are important. We need to feel that we make a difference to the world and are a vital part of something, no matter how small.

We have to realize that every individual is unique and special and that everyone needs and deserves respect. In other words we have to adjust our attitude towards people.

All it takes is a word of appreciation, encouragement, acknowledgement, an action to let people know they matter, a compliment, or admiring them for a talent or quality they have. There are so many different ways to let people know they are important.

Kind words can be short and easy to speak,
but their echoes are truly endless.
Mother Teresa

Sometimes all we need is for someone to believe in us. We're generally so focused on our weaknesses that it's easier for someone else to recognize and point out our strengths. The amazing thing is, often this simple act helps us to discover talents we never thought or knew we had. Thus positively uplifting one another can have life-long and life-changing affects.

"I Believe I Can!"

I fell,
you were there to catch me and offer support.
I cried,
you were there to wipe my tears and encourage me.
I failed,
you were there to help me.
I succeeded,
you were there to praise me.
When there was laughter,
you laughed with me, not at me.
I said I can't,
you said I could.
For all these reasons, today
"I believe I can!"

Sally Eichhorst

Chapter 8

Stop Criticising And Start Reinforcing!

(Area 4)

Pay no attention to what the critics say;
no statue has ever been erected to a critic.

Jean Sibelius

A herd of reindeer was crossing a river when two of the weaker reindeer were swept downstream by a powerful current. Although the other reindeer battled, they safely reached the other side. They knew how strong the current was as they themselves had barely made it across, so they all agreed that the two stragglers were as good as dead. In a chorus they all shouted downstream to the two battling reindeer that they might as well give up. They would never make it and should rather relax and stop fighting it as they were just prolonging their agony.

But the two struggling reindeer did all they could to keep their heads above water and swim against the current. The other reindeer kept yelling for them to stop fighting the current, as there was nothing they could do. They should just resign themselves to the fact that they were as good as dead. Eventually one of the reindeer started to listen to what the others were shouting. He resigned himself to the fact that he was as good as dead and simply gave up. The powerful current immediately swept him away and drowned him.

The other struggling reindeer fought with all his might against the current. He frantically kicked his legs and urged his body to pull out all the stops to save him. All the other reindeer again shouted to him to just give in, as no amount of struggling would help him. The reindeer tried even harder to push himself to his limits and to the disbelief of all the others, he finally made it to safety. When he reached the others, they asked him, 'Didn't you hear what we were shouting to you?' The reindeer sheepishly admitted that the reason why he has always been a little bit of a straggler is that he is almost deaf. You see, he couldn't hear what they were shouting to him. He believed that they were actually encouraging him not to give up and to fight on the entire time.

What is the deep and powerful message within this story? BE VERY CAREFUL OF WHAT YOU SAY! A simple word of encouragement to someone who really needs it could be the very thing that helps them to rise above their situation and make it through a difficult patch. However, any destructive word, maybe a word to discourage or criticize someone who is already feeling down or in a pickle, could be the very thing that takes them over the edge and makes them give up on life.

Words have the power to either destroy or strengthen.
Choose them well
and never let them destroy the life you are building.

Warren & Sally

Nobody likes to be criticised. Remember the last time you were criticised? Chances are feelings ran high and even if you were in the wrong, you probably found yourself defending your point of view to the death. No one likes to be told they're wrong or to be put down and it is quite a normal reaction for people to counter-attack, whether they're in the wrong or not. So if you don't enjoy being criticised, then make an effort not to criticise others.

With criticism, often nothing good is accomplished and a lot of damage can be done. Be careful of what you say to others and don't allow what others say to you, to affect you negatively.

Stop criticising and start reinforcing! In other words use encouragement and praise rather than destructive criticism. Don't concentrate on what people are doing wrong, but rather on what they are doing right.

You can tell more about a person by what he says about others than you can by what others say about him.

Unknown

Ask yourself this, if we were to pay you fifty cents for every kind word you ever spoke and collect fifty cents for every unkind word you ever spoke, would you be rich or poor?

Chapter 9

Become Genuinely Interested In Others.

(Area5)

You can make more friends in two months
by becoming interested in other people
than you can in two years
by trying to get other people interested in you.

Dale Carnegie

Isn't it amazing that years of education are spent on teaching us to read, write and speak effectively, but what about listening? In most cases, no one teaches us to listen properly with the result that many people do not know how. It is a statistical fact that most of us spend more of our lives listening than we do reading, writing or speaking. So it stands to reason that we should develop this skill until it becomes a talent. Many of the world's most successful businessmen and leaders attribute their success to good listening skills and therefore effective communication and negotiation. It's amazing how much information you can gather about people and the depth and understanding you can reach, if only you take the time and effort to really listen.

We know you all think you're good listeners, but in reality, it's a rare talent. Just think back to a recent debate, argument or disagreement you had with someone. Now be honest, you were primarily interested in getting your point or side of the story across, not so? Whether it meant raising your voice louder, talking more or constantly interrupting the other person. Yes, of course you heard their point or side of the story, but did you really listen? In most cases, probably not.

In fact, most of us hardly listen to a word the other person is saying, when trying to get our point across. Why? Well, isn't it true that whilst they're speaking, instead of listening, you're just watching for every opportunity to dive in there and get all your points across? You're also thinking about what you're going to say next and lining up all the things you want to say, like ammunition.

The thing is, we often think we're being receptive, when in actual fact most of the time, our minds are so full of our own beliefs, opinions, judgements, morals, values, and knowledge, resulting in no new space for input. So we may very well hear what the other has to say, but it's not sinking in and won't sink in until we can open our minds and create a little room for new ideas, viewpoints and beliefs. Only, through really listening can you learn, accept and discover from others as well as understand them and where they're coming from, thereby avoiding conflict.

Nature gave us one tongue and two ears
so we could hear twice as much as we speak

Epictetus

A friend who is involved in a great deal of marriage counselling once told us that most marriage problems are really communication problems and often it is more a listening problem than anything else. A lot of selective listening takes place – listening only to what you want and then switching off to the rest or switching off to things that one feels uncomfortable with. This leads to a great deal of misunderstanding and conflict. Sound familiar? He often advises couples to start really listening to one another more often and not only when it suits them. Listen and learn!

Be a good listener.
Your ears will never get you in trouble.

Frank Tyger

At the end of the day, it doesn't matter what field you're in, what position you're in and who you are. What matters is that you start paying more attention to everyone by really concentrating. Never assume you know what people want, think or feel.

A good friend of ours, Joe, has his own successful small business. Several years ago his business was battling, with high staff turnover, low staff morale and low productivity levels. After analysing the situation, Joe came to the realization that his lack of interest and attention was actually part of the problem. So he started to pay more attention to his staff as well as his clients. Even though he was exceptionally busy, he squeezed in at least an hour every day to go around and speak to every member of his staff. During these talks he would discuss their needs, interests and wants, also finding out what their goals and aspirations were.

By paying attention to his staff, they suddenly viewed him differently and also paid more attention to him. His staff turnover dropped dramatically as they became more loyal and committed. There was an increased sense of responsibility, as they did not want to let him down. There was also a renewed understanding amongst everyone and communication channels were opened, resulting in minimal misunderstandings. Staff willingly went the extra mile and productivity levels soared.

Joe applied the same concept to his clients and again the response was unbelievable. His interest in them was rewarded by more business as he strengthened relationships and gathered leads and information he would otherwise have missed out on.

All in all, the simple act of making an effort to understand people better by getting to know their needs, interests and wants had turned Joe's business around into the successful business it is today.

The true measure of a man,
is how he treats someone
who can do him absolutely no good.

Unknown

People will only listen to you if they feel you are genuinely hearing them. So learn to concentrate and pay attention. Most importantly, develop a genuine interest in all you meet.

Part 3

Conquer The Big '3'

Far From Done

Going for a song, a life that's gone wrong.
I don't need it anymore. It's become such a bore.

Nothing ever goes right. It just seems an uphill fight.
Surely it can't be fair, that I see problems everywhere.

So I'm throwing in the towel, because this life's just been foul.
I can't face another day, with things not going my way.

Good-bye everyone. This Life and me are done!
'Wait,' shouts Life.
'Before you take me with you, just allow me this one chance,
to prove to you that you and I deserve a second glance.'

'Look a little closer and you are sure to see
all the good things deep down in me.
I have so much to offer, all I need is time,
to prove to you that together we can do just fine.'

'Focus on the good in me and it's a fact you'll soon see,
that the good out weighs the bad
and I'm actually the best deal you've ever had.'

'You and I are far from done
whilst we can still have so much fun!'

Sally Eichhorst

Chapter 10

Conquer Fear

" One can never hope to discover new oceans
if they don't have the courage to lose sight of the shore. "
Unknown

It was late, dark and secluded as the man walked briskly home. An unmistakable rustle and commotion from the bushes stopped him in his tracks. He listened intently for what seemed like a lifetime but was really mere seconds. He could distinguish the muffled screams and frantic struggling of a woman and the low guttural bark of a man. Then a tearing sound - perhaps a blouse being torn open? He identified a single word, which seemed to echo endlessly in his ears - 'Help.'

Panic stricken, it dawned on him that a woman was being attacked right there, at that very minute and right in front of him.

Now what? What should he do? What could he do? He was not a big man and by no means strong or athletic. Surely if he got involved he would be hurt, possibly even killed. If he were killed or badly hurt, what would become of his family? Maybe he should rather run to the nearest phone, call the police and then come back with help. But then it may be too late!

Fear seemed to paralyse him in a vice-like grip and seconds

seemed like an eternity before he made up his mind. To conquer his fear, he must take action, and take it fast before he changed his mind. He simply could not walk away even if it was for the life of a stranger. He would have to face his fear by tackling it head on. How could he live with himself if this unknown woman could have been saved, if only he'd acted with force and speed?

Once he had decided to act and even put his life on the line, he seemed to gain courage and found an inner strength so powerful that he suddenly felt confident and capable of helping this stranger.

He rushed through the bushes and charged the woman's attacker, pulling him off her and wrestling him to the ground. A vicious struggle ensued until the attacker managed to escape.

In all this time, the woman sat crouched in a protective ball with her face buried in her lap, rocking and sobbing softly. He hadn't been able to get a clear look at her and still couldn't as it was too dark. His heart went out to her as he sensed her shock and fear.

He was afraid to add to her fear by approaching her immediately and decided to rather say some comforting words to relax her and gain her trust. "Are you okay? I'm here to help you. You're safe now. No one can harm you anymore," he said gently and soothingly.

The sobbing stopped and a long silence followed. Then the unknown woman asked with amazement and relief, 'Dad, is that really you?'

Shocked and choked with emotion and disbelief, the man

watched as his youngest daughter, Kathy came forward, blouse torn, body bruised, eyes wide with shock, face swollen and red from a torrent of shed tears.

This man's selfless act of putting his own life on the line to save the life of a stranger went well rewarded, as the life he ended up saving was in fact that of his very own daughter. **We all have to make some difficult choices in life, but most importantly we all have to live with the consequences**. Imagine this man's consequences if he had let his fears paralyse his efforts and stop him from taking action to help the girl.

Our fears can literally immobilize us. They often stop us from taking positive action and limit our lives in ways we can't begin to imagine.

We think fear is a signal to withdraw when it is really a sign that we are already withdrawing too much

Thaddeus Golas

Dare to walk the plank

To dare is to lose one's footing momentarily.
To not dare is to lose oneself.

Soren Kierkegaard

When we mention FEAR in our seminars, most of the attendees believe that they have no fear and even if they did, it can't possibly limit them in any way. We then conduct a little experiment to prove them wrong.

On the floor, we place a long, solid, wooden plank from one side of the room to the other. The plank is only just wide enough for them to comfortably walk across without touching the ground.

We ask everyone present to walk across. Each and every one of the attendees happily and successfully walks from one side of the plank to the other. Then we elevate the plank to half a metre from the ground and again ask everyone present to walk across. Still everyone easily walks across. However, when we raise the plank to twice the average ceiling height (a good couple of metres, that only a trapeze artist would feel at home on) – what do you think happens?

At ground level and at a half a metre, there is no risk of getting hurt if you fall, so everyone walks across happily without falling. However, at twice the average ceiling height, there is most certainly a risk of serious damage should one fall. Suddenly, the fear of falling comes into play. Even though everyone knows that they can easily walk across the plank, as they'd successfully proven it on two occasions, they now have serious doubts about their ability to make it and on most occasions all of them do not even attempt to do the last plank walk!

So what happens when some brave souls decide to go for it? Most will fall! Why? Because they will be focused on their fear of falling, their fear of taking this unnecessary risk, their fear of height and open space all around them and last but not least, their fear of getting hurt. They become so focused on their fear that they start to question their ability to make it, eventually believing that they won't and thus falling.

There will be those who do actually make it across. Why?

Because they are focused on making it and believe that because they did it before, it can easily be done again, no matter what the risk. **There is no fear to limit them, only belief to guide them**.

In the same respect, if we have a wonderful business opportunity, which can make a great deal of money and holds absolutely no risk, we guarantee that most people will jump at it. However, if the same opportunity involves a substantial risk, most people will turn down the opportunity. The fear of taking risks, fear of loss of security, fear of failure should things go sour, fear of criticism by others should things go wrong, all come into play. People just don't realize how fear affects their decisions and often limits them from taking up opportunities, doing what they really want and getting what they really want.

The Chinese character for 'crisis' is a combination of two words: 'danger' and 'opportunity', So see the positive potential of your next fearful situation.

Can You Sing?

Use what talent you possess: the woods would be very silent if no birds sang except those that sang best.

Henry Van Dyke

One of our favourite questions at our motivational seminars is ***'Who can sing?'*** What do you think the response is? It's amazing how many people suddenly deny outright their ability to sing! It's very rarely that we get a raised hand and that is usually only because he or she sings professionally.

Well, the truth of the matter is - WE CAN ALL SING! From a young age until our dying day, we can sing, no matter who we are. We didn't ask these people if they could sing well or in tune and we certainly didn't ask them to stand up or come forward to sing at that very moment. All we asked was, 'Who can sing?'

You see, the fear of criticism rears its ugly head, causing them to be too scared to admit that they can sing, in case they make a spectacle of themselves if indeed they're asked to sing.

This is so typical of most people. They would rather say that they can't do something and not even try because they fear criticism from others should they fail or prove to be below average.

Now when we asked a group of pre-schoolers the same question, what do you think the response was? They all jumped up and down in their seats ready to sing their favourite song at the top of their voices. Why? Because their fear of criticism, failure and rejection amongst others, has not developed yet.

If a baby was born with fear, it would never learn to walk, talk, thirst for knowledge or attempt to learn new skills. Picture it - a baby tries to walk and it falls. If it feared failure or criticism, it may never try again. It is the lack of fear that enables them to learn and grow. A child's innocence is its key to self-growth.

Observe most young children and it will become clear that they are brilliant and creative thinkers, hungry for knowledge, new experiences and new friends. Everyday, they face the unknown head on as they learn, smell, taste, see and hear new things, breathing and taking in all life has to offer.

As we grow older, our fears grow too. Some of us are even encouraged and taught not to take risks and become afraid of challenges. These same people would argue that they have become wiser with age. Is this really the case? If you never take any risks you will never reap the fruitful benefits and rewards usually attached. If you become complacent and fear change, you will crumble in the face of any challenge and will never truly enjoy self-fulfilment.

Think of your own little pre-schoolers, your own kids when they were pre-schoolers or just those that you know or have seen and celebrate the fact that they have got the right idea about life. Their self-esteem is at a peak and their thirst for life and knowledge is boundless. Their fearlessness is their key to growth. They do plenty of things every day, which are new to them and even potentially hazardous, yet they feed on these experiences instead of fearing them.

Why don't you do just one thing that scares you every day. It doesn't have to be anything radical like jumping from a plane or running with the bulls. It could be anything you feel uncomfortable doing, incapable of doing or afraid to do. See it as a challenge a day to get the old child-like spirit of adventure sparked off again. For some it may be as simple as changing a lifelong routine, breaking a habit, trying out a new activity or simply standing up to someone. Just do it! Once a day, face a fear, no matter how little and soon, fear will be a thing of the past.

You gain strength, courage, and confidence
by every experience in which you really stop to look fear in the face.
You must do the thing, which you think you cannot do.

Eleanor Roosevelt

The Paralysing Effect Of Fear - by Sally

It took place many years ago, when I was still a tiny tot (nothing much has changed) in junior school. I was a good swimmer and Backstroke was my speciality. I won every race, often lapping other swimmers and was full of confidence in my ability.

My Dad then decided to take some time off work to come and watch me swim, as he had heard so much about my talent for Backstroke. Proud and boastful, he sat amongst all the ladies and spread the word about his brilliant daughter who had an extraordinary talent for Backstroke, always winning by far and even lapping the last few stragglers.

As he crooned and everyone 'oohed' and 'aahed' about his fabulous daughter, yours truly suddenly found herself doubting her ability. I knew I was good and had proven it over and over again, but now my Dad was here watching me. What if I didn't win? What if he didn't think I was good enough or fast enough? What if I let him down?

Well, I was so focused on my fear of criticism from my Dad and my fear of failure that I became almost paralysed by it. The starter gun went off and I didn't! To be exact, before I had even swum a metre, my right arm got caught up in the ropes that separate the lanes and for the life of me, I just couldn't free myself. There I thrashed around like a fish out of water and I think you've all guessed it; I came stone last!

My Dad admitted many years later that he had cringed with embarrassment, wanting to melt away into his seat. When the ladies asked where his daughter was, he lied and said he couldn't see me - perhaps I was sick?

I was sick alright - sick with fear. I had allowed fear to limit me; to literally paralyse me! In this way, fear limits so many people from really doing what they want and performing at their peak.

How many of you have allowed fear to limit you and literally paralyse you in this way?

There are so many people out there, who permit family, friends and the general public to influence them to such an extent that they never live their lives as they truly want to. They allow these people to make decisions for them, because they fear criticism, failure and rejection amongst other things.

The moon could not go on shining
if it paid any attention to the little dogs that bark at it

Anonymous

The world is full of people whose lives are limited by fear. Amongst these are those who don't study further, don't try for a new and more prospective job, won't accept a promotion or take any chances in business and there are even those who will remain in a failed and unhappy marriage for the rest of their lives. All this as a result of some limiting fear.

You're Never Too Old

" Never complain about growing old,
Because so many never get the chance!"

Unknown

Sometimes we fear that we are too old to start again. We fear that it is too late to change anything about our present situation. How wrong can people be?

Janine Williams, a partner in one of our businesses and a good friend, recently decided to supplement her studies further. As she stood in a queue at UNISA to register for this four-year degree, she looked around her and suddenly felt a little old. 'I wondered if perhaps it wasn't too late in life to study again and to change into a new area of academic focus. Four years is a long time and I would be in my late thirties, creeping up on the big forty, by the time I completed the degree,' she told us.

Then she noticed a little old lady standing in the same queue as her. 'I got chatting to the lady only to find that this **ninety four year old** lady was registering for the very same four year degree as me! This little old lady was totally unconcerned with her age and didn't even question that she would be around to complete the degree or put it to use. She had a thirst for knowledge and she was quenching her thirst, regardless of age.' Janine told us.

Next time you fear that you're too old to tackle something or start over, remember this little ninety four year old lady.

Don't fear age for fear ages you!

Sally &Warren

One of our employees needed a lift home one day and we volunteered to drop her off. She was a jolly woman in her early sixties and lived with her husband and her father.

When we walked into her house the first thing that struck us was the beautiful pictures that decorated the walls of the house.

We could see that they were by the same artist and asked her where she'd got them from? She proudly explained that her father was the artist. What astonished us was that he'd only started painting in his eighties. Before that he had never picked up a paintbrush in his life. He was a bricklayer by trade and never realised he had this talent until he had time to discover it. He was making more money in a week from his paintings than he'd made in a month when he was working as a bricklayer.

So Fear Not!

Shoot for the moon
Even if you miss it you will land among the stars

Les Brown

It seems that most of us have forgotten that we've all failed on numerous occasions. Just think back to when you were a baby. Your first few attempted steps were probably a walking disaster. Your first attempts at speech, probably laughable. Learning to swim was probably more a case of trying not to drown. Reading and writing certainly were not skills you mastered on your first attempt. It all came right through trial and error like most things in life.

English novelist John Creasey received 753 rejection slips before he successfully published 564 books. So rather worry about the chances you miss when you don't even try.

Unfortunately, most of us fear loss much more than we desire gain. Most of us work much harder hanging for dear life onto what we already have, maintaining our present standards. We do this, rather than taking risks to get what we really and truly want from our lives, thereby raising our standards. To succeed, we must learn to overcome this fear of loss. We have to realize that there is no true security in anything. If we want a better life, we have to take our chances. We must make a decision to stop fearing loss and to start focusing on what it is we want from life.

Love and risk being hurt.
Give and risk being taken for granted.
Help and risk involvement.
Speak out and risk disagreement.
Be different and risk criticism.
Make a valid attempt and risk failure.
Climb and risk falling.
Truly live and risk dying.

Life is a risk!
Those who avoid all risks are avoiding Life itself.
Indeed Life's greatest risk is not to risk at all!

Sally Eichhorst

Chapter 11

Conquer Worry

" Worry does not empty tomorrow of its sorrow;
it empties today of its strength."

Unknown

Michelle puts worry into perspective

I woke up this morning and as I stared at the pale, familiar image in the bathroom mirror, I noticed a blind pimple on the end of my nose. There it was, standing out like a lone, but distinct flagpole on Mount Everest. I tried to hide it as best I could, but worried nevertheless that everyone I came into contact with would be drawn to that spot on my nose and have a conversation with it, instead of me. So there was my first worry. Then came my outfit. I worried whether it was really suitable for this particular interview. Was I overdressed or underdressed? I then worried about whether the person I was to interview would like me and open up to me. Would I do a good job and be able to create an interesting enough story? Worry, worry, worry! This was a typical morning for me, full of trivial worries, which I obsessed over. It seemed I was never able to relax, as there was always this cloud of anxiety hovering over me.

So here I was worrying myself into a state again for no

apparent reason. I wasn't sure what this interview was all about, as my boss had rushed in the previous afternoon and asked me to take her place. She said it would make a great story but unfortunately she was too busy and anyway she felt I would benefit from the experience. All I was given was a name, time and a meeting place. John at the House of Coffee in town at 9 a.m.

On the way to this meeting place I worried whether I would find John and worried that he may not want to speak to me as he was expecting my boss. Was I good enough to do as professional a job as she would have? I thought about my job as a journalist and worried about whether it was what I really wanted to do with my life. Would I ever earn enough to live the way I wanted to and do all the things I wanted to?

I arrived at the designated meeting place at 8.50 a.m. and as I entered I was bathed in the delightfully cosy and warm aroma of coffee hanging lazily in the air. After scanning my surroundings, I came to the conclusion that John had not yet arrived. There was only a young couple whispering sweet nothings into one another's ears and an old lady sipping a cup of coffee over the morning paper.

I ordered a cappuccino and settled in at a booth facing the doorway so I could spot John the moment he arrived. Patience is not one of my virtues and waiting just allowed me to worry further. As I was undoubtedly about to launch into another list of worries, something caught my eye.

Just outside the entrance, leaning against the window, was a man I had often seen around town. In fact, he had been there when I entered the coffee shop, but I hadn't paid him much attention as I was focused on looking for John, the mystery man who I was supposed to interview.

The only reason I had ever noticed this man leaning against the window was because he was a cripple and his only mode of transport was a dilapidated old skateboard. I'd seen him pushing his way around town on gloved hands whilst his crippled and useless stump-like legs remained limp and lifeless on the skateboard.

Thinking back, I remembered seeing him around town often and what struck me now was the fact that he had always been genuinely smiling on all those occasions and yes, right now there was also a huge, happy grin on his face, stretching from ear to ear. Maybe he's not only badly crippled, but also a little dumb, I thought. Surely he has nothing to smile about in his life, so he must be slightly retarded to be looking so happy with everything.

Suddenly our eyes met and before I could guiltily avert my gaze, I realized that he was pushing his way into the coffee shop and heading in my direction. 'Oh, no!' I thought, he's actually coming right at me. What could he possibly want? Money of course! What if I can't get rid of him and he messes up my whole interview with John? I really do feel sorry for him, but now is just not`the right time or place. I reached into my bag and scrabbled around for some small change to offer him. As I looked up from my purse, triumphantly clutching some change, I was startled by a softly spoken male voice asking politely, 'Are you perhaps Mrs. Norton?' 'You're John?' was my shocked and embarrassed reply as the grinning cripple nodded in response.

There we sat chatting for two glorious hours. Who would have guessed that these would be two of the most important and enriching hours of my life? John turned out to be anything but retarded or stupid. The truth is he was actually quite bright with a wonderful sense of humour and a contagious smile.

It turns out that John is always smiling because he is genuinely happy. Here is a man who is badly crippled, illiterate due to lack of education, unemployed and reduced to begging, yet he has no worries and is happy and content with the life he has. Not because he is stupid or knows no better, but because he chooses to make the most of what he does have and can do. What he does have is a skateboard to get around on and a friendly, likeable and happy disposition, which endears people to him and makes them want to help him.

I admit I was totally taken aback and fascinated by this humble man. Not once did he harp on about the negatives of his life or the unfairness of his situation. Instead, he pointed out all the things he had to live for and was grateful and happy about. Worries especially, were things he never wasted his time and energy on. He simply didn't see the point of upsetting himself over things he could either do nothing about or things that may never happen.

I suddenly became profoundly aware of all my days, weeks, months and years of endless worrying. Thinking back to my recent worries this morning, I was overwhelmed by guilt and embarrassment. My major concern for the day up until this point had been the pimple on the end of my nose. How pathetic!

Simply talking to John for two hours had opened up a new world for me. A world free of worry. I realized that all of us, especially myself, have to put our worries into perspective. The moment we start to worry, we should think of those who are far worse off than us and truly have major problems, which they would willingly trade for ours in a split-second.

Often the things we worry about are things we cannot change or are simply trivial things, which certainly don't warrant upsetting ourselves over.

Worry is like a rocking chair that gives you something to do but never gets you anywhere

J Jelinek

Now, every time I start to worry, I think of John, who in my eyes should have a mountain of worries considering his circumstances. Then I think of my situation. I have a home, a car, a job, a supportive family, I'm well educated and want for nothing. What could I possibly worry about? So worry for me is a thing of the past and I hope that my story has encouraged you to think twice before you worry.

'What am I worrying about?'

Worry is wasting today's time cluttering up tomorrow's opportunities with yesterday's troubles

Unknown

Stop right now and ask yourself, 'What am I worrying about? Is this thing I'm worrying about really worth the stress it is giving me?' Chances are you'll probably find that it's something trivial and unimportant. So don't waste your precious time and energy on worrying. It simply isn't worth it!

How to avoid worry!

When we are busy at work with our mind full of the challenges of the day, it is difficult for the 'worry bug' to settle in. It is when the mind is free from the day's work and we are doing nothing in particular or lying in bed with the lights out that the 'worry bug' has its chance to creep in. We start to worry about things that have gone wrong during the day and could still go wrong, what we should have or shouldn't have said to others and whether we are getting anywhere in life.

So how do you avoid worrying? Simple! An excellent way to avoid worrying is to allow yourself no time for worrying. In other words, keep your mind occupied. What you must also understand is that there is a 99% chance that your worries will never become a reality. So don't waste your time and energy worrying about something until it happens. Just this small change can create a major improvement in all areas of your life.

"I am an old man and have a great many troubles,
But most of them never happened."

Mark Twain

Most of what we worry about comes from our imagination and not from our physical existence. Look back over the years and you too will realize that most of your worries were only a figment of your imagination.

Eliminate senseless worry

Worry tries to cross a bridge before you come to it
Anonymous

Of all the things you worry about 99% will definitely never happen.

Of this 99%

- 50% is worrying about the past, which is unalterable.
- 27% is worrying about what others say or think about you. These criticisms, on the most part are incorrect and made by people who have nothing better to say or are trying to make themselves feel better.
- 22% is worrying about your health, which is only aggravated further by worry.

Only 1% represents those worthwhile worries, which we should be concerned about. These are the only worries we should spend our time thinking about and then taking action to do something about.

Today is the tomorrow you worried about yesterday.
Unknown

Chapter 12

Conquer Depression

People are just about as happy as they make up their minds to be.
Abraham Lincoln

Three choices you must make to conquer depression:

1. Choose the positive interpretation of any experience.

Dwelling on negative and traumatic experiences is often a sure way to fall headlong into a nasty pit of depression. Sally vividly remembers an ugly experience she had several years ago in Israel.

'I had innocently gone on a date with a guy who seemed to be a gentleman. I only later discovered that there lurked a monster within. Once we were safely back at my place, attempting to keep the evening innocent, I rejected any advances and was suddenly met with the transformation of gentleman to angry monster. All 5 ft 2 of me was suddenly confronted with this ferocious 6ft 4 giant who was obviously not used to and certainly not fond of rejection.

He proceeded to airlift me and hurl me across the room. My back hit the wall with a crunch and I crumpled into a sorry heap on the floor. As the giant advanced, ready to finish off what he had started, I remembered in that split second, how often I had wondered how I would react if I was ever attacked. Would I fight back or would I just freeze with shock? Maybe I'd scream or just run like crazy as soon as I saw even a hint of escape. Would I now become yet another of the World's victims of crime? Would this experience ruin my life if indeed I were still around afterwards? So what did I do? I did what I least expected myself to do and in a crazy sort of way I learnt more then about myself than through any other experience.

Terrified and really wanting to melt away into the wall behind me, I surprised myself by standing up straight, puffing out my chest and pushing back my shoulders in an attempt to make myself look as big and foreboding as possible. I was further amazed to discover that my terror was replaced by explosive anger as I charged headlong for my attacker. I literally saw red, as they say and counter-attacked like an injured animal. I was outraged at being physically violated and made to feel like a victim. 'I'd rather go out fighting than let him get the better of me', I thought.

I believe he was surprised by my ferocious counter-attack and total disregard for my own safety, not to mention my disrespect for his obvious size and strength advantage.

Taken totally off guard, the 'giant' obviously had second thoughts as he started doing some serious back-peddling to avoid my advance. Enraged, I pounced on him, screeching, scratching, biting, tearing, kicking, punching – you get the idea. Some friends heard the commotion and had to literally tear me off him.

Suffice it to say that at the end of the day, I believe that he came out of it worse off than I did.

This is a negative experience, which could easily have had a lifelong detrimental impact on me. I could have clung to all the worst interpretations like, 'I'm not safe anywhere,' 'I can't trust anyone,' 'It's only a matter of time before I'll again be faced with some form of violent crime,' 'Why me?' It's so easy to start thinking all these negative thoughts and as you dwell on them, you keep finding new ones to add on until you're in a deep pit of depression, surrounded with negative thoughts.

Life is about perception and interpretation. It's not the event or experience, which has value and can cause you to become negative and depressed. It is how you choose to interpret the experience, which gives it value and determines your reaction.

After this experience, I thought long and hard about the whole episode and how I was going to let it affect me. I realized that although this was possibly one of the worst experiences of my life, it had taught me more about myself than anything else that had previously happened to me. I had discovered a strength of character I never knew I had, a fighting spirit which refused to be the victim. I felt that I had learnt a valuable lesson with regards to safety and trust. An obvious lesson was that I never wanted to be in the same or a similar situation again.'

We are like tea bags
We don't know our own strength until we're in hot water.
Sis. Busche

Often we learn the most about ourselves and life in general from our darkest hours. When we encounter negative experiences, we have to somehow look for positives or rather things we can learn from the experiences and take those lessons with us through life, forgetting the rest. There are so many different interpretations to a single experience. You choose how you let experiences affect you by your interpretation of them and the value you give to them. If you want to live a happy and stress-free life, you must find the most positive interpretation of every negative experience you encounter and put value only on the lessons learnt.

Whether you lose money at the races, drive into your neighbour's Mercedes, fail an exam, get dumped by a loved one or your house burns down, remember that it is not these things that make you depressed; it is how or what you think about them that makes you depressed. In other words it is how you interpret the situation.

Yes, we all have our down times, when our good feelings are eroded by circumstances and events, but we can avoid falling headlong into depression by forcing ourselves to concentrate on the brighter side of life and situations.

There are many terrible things that most of us will encounter in life. Although we may feel that we have no control whatsoever over them, we must remember that we can control the most important thing – how we will let these things affect our lives.

2. Choose happiness over depression

"Remember happiness doesn't depend upon who you are or what you have; it depends solely upon what you think."

Dale Carnegie

You create your own depression as well as all the other results

in your life, through the thoughts you dwell upon, your behaviour and the actions you take. There is no other way!
You are what you think and ultimately your thoughts will make up your life. If you think miserable thoughts, you will be miserable. If you think exciting and motivating thoughts you will be enthusiastic and motivated. So if you think depressing thoughts, you will be depressed. **What you think, is of vital importance to ascertain not only who you are, but also how you are.** What you must realise is that unless you suffer from a chemical imbalance that has to be treated medically, you can help yourself beat depression.

To beat depression you should not only focus on thinking happy and positive thoughts, but also distance yourself from those that put you down, as well as those negative people whose influence so easily rubs off on you. You should also take charge of your life by not harping on hurtful memories of the past.

Sadly, there are many people who tend to hang onto traumas and tragedies for as long as possible, dragging out their misery for years. These people are only punishing themselves more by refusing to let go of the past. It's a shame! You only have one life so why waste so much of it being depressed? You have to learn to let go of the past and get on with the act of living your life to its fullest. Go through that old closet that is your mind and do some spring-cleaning. Throw out all those burdensome bad memories and experiences you've been hoarding. Rather make room for better memories and experiences still to come in the future.

The solution is to make a point of always surrounding yourself with positive people, thinking only positive thoughts, remembering only positive memories and focusing on where you want to go in life.

" The happiest people don't necessarily have the best of everything, They just make the best of everything."

Unknown

Depression vs. happiness - It's your choice...

Happiness, that 'elusive thing' we're all after, which somehow manages to slip from the grasp of most, escaping them at every attempt of capture. There are those who travel to all corners of the earth in the hope of finding it. There are those who buy bigger houses, cars and toys to capture it. There are those who drink more and party harder to feel it even for a fleeting moment. There are those whose whole lives revolve around a lover or spouse, relying solely on them to supply the happiness they crave.

Then there are countless people who believe in the theory of 'happiness comes later, when I have done this or that, or when I have overcome this or that.' It is no wonder then, that happiness eludes most, as people are searching for it in the wrong places and for the wrong reasons, setting all sorts of prerequisites for its existence. Well, it cannot be found or simply appear from nowhere and it certainly does not just happen to you.

Happiness is something very personal, that each and every one of us is capable of. Achieving happiness is not a matter of luck, possessions, ability, money, fame or glory. It is not up to someone or some event to come along and make you happy. It's all up to you! You don't have to wait for anything to make you happy. **You can be happy right now by making a firm**

decision to choose to be happy.

Really work at convincing yourself that you are happy and you will be. Think only happy thoughts and you will attract only happy experiences and manufacture a happy and healthy state of mind. Do this often enough and it will soon become second nature; you will naturally be happy. You will have succeeded at something many geniuses, heroes, famous stars and millionaires have failed at.

Happiness is a state of mind. It is a proven fact that happiness does not follow naturally with the acquisition of wealth, material goods or fame. Many make the mistake of associating happiness with money, power and glory. Acquiring any one or more of these may not lead directly to happiness. You must be happy within yourself.

It's great to have money, but if it is happiness you're truly after it simply can't be bought. Research led by professors from the London School of Economics has conclusively proved that money can buy everything but happiness. A World Happiness Survey led to the eye-opening discovery that Bangladesh, which is one of the poorest places in the world, is in fact the happiest nation in the world. It was found that people in most rich countries such as Switzerland, Japan, Canada and Austria amongst others are far less happy than people in poorer countries like India, Armenia, the Dominican Republic, Ghana and Croatia. This is certainly food for thought and should be chewed on for awhile before it is digested and forgotten!

We would be happier with what we have if we weren't so unhappy about what we don't' have

Frank A. Clark

You should also forget about relying on something or someone for your happiness. For true, long lasting happiness you can rely only on yourself. So choose to be happy now and fill your mind with your reasons for happiness. Do the things that make you feel good and learn to see the bright side of life, filling your world with laughter. Remember, 'He who laughs, lasts!' Why not also devote some time and energy to making others happy and it will return to you tenfold.

The happiness that eludes most of us, is in fact well within everyone's grasp, if only they choose to create it and attract it.

The foolish man seeks happiness in the distance,
the wise grows it under his feet.
James Oppenheim

3. Choose to see problems as opportunities to grow

The block of granite which is an obstacle in the pathway of the weak,
becomes a stepping-stone in the pathway of the strong
Thomas Carlyle

Legend has it that there once lived a wise old King who was looking for a new advisor. This was a position of great importance and required a special kind of man. The wise old King had a plan. He had a gigantic rock inconveniently placed in the middle of the roadway to his Kingdom. He then hid in nearby bushes so that he would have a clear view of all that passed and came across the obstacle.

A number of highly respected officials came past. They cursed and groaned about the state of the road, complaining that the King should take better care of his roads and of them. None of them even attempted to move the great rock and all walked around it. Wealthy merchants and others of position and standing did the same. Most complained and yet not one did anything about the obstacle in question. They all walked around it.

Just when the King was losing hope, a young peasant walked past laden with baskets of fruit to sell at the market. He approached the rock and without hesitation, placed his baskets down and attempted to move the great rock from the road. It wasn't an easy task and took much effort and some time before the peasant managed to successfully move the rock aside.

The King was thrilled. He summoned the peasant to his chambers and pronounced him the new King's Advisor, easily the most respected and sought after post of all officials. Why? Because it took a special kind of man not to complain about problems or obstacles. It took a special kind of man not to blame others for obstacles or problems in their path. Indeed it took a special kind of man to rather take action and remove the obstacle without hesitation instead of walking away from it or avoiding it.

When the wise old King made the announcement to his Kingdom, he told them that every obstacle, more often than not presents a hidden opportunity. An obstacle is a challenge to either learn from or improve one's condition, even if the reward is not always clear or visible. The new King's Advisor had learned what many never understand and was thus a special kind of man.

Think about it - what 'huge rocks' or obstacles that are in your life at the moment, may actually be hidden nuggets of opportunity for you to gain from?

Everyone has their share of problems...

A friend of ours attended an interesting stress management seminar a number of years ago. Upon entering the conference room, each person was asked to write down two of their most pressing personal problems on a small piece of paper. No names were mentioned and all the papers were tossed into a hat.

Although curious, most of the people including our friend, soon forgot about the hat and its contents as the seminar progressed.

The aim of the seminar was to get people to interact and to open up to one another about the stress they were under. Soon everyone was unloading and sharing a sad tale with the rest and it seemed no one was immune from some sort of major hardship or problem.

There were some who had lost loved ones and others who had lost jobs. There were those who were going through a bad divorce while others were lonely and depressed. A few were coping with seriously ill loved ones and then there were those who were faced with terminal illness themselves. Some were battling to make ends meet and others had lost their businesses. A handful were victims of emotional or physical abuse and one or two were recovering from some form of addiction.

Then out came the hat everyone had momentarily forgotten about. Each person was to pick out a piece of paper from the hat. Everyone was told that this was a lucky draw and could be their lucky day as they could trade in their problems for the one's they chose from the hat.

Our friend took one look at the two problems scribbled on the paper she'd chosen and announced loudly that she would much rather have her own problems back. Many others were doing the same and the general consensus seemed to be that everyone would rather deal with their own problems.

The conclusion to this little exercise was that their own problems now seemed a lot less difficult and a lot more manageable in light of everyone else's problems. They all came to understand and appreciate that often the hardships or worries they endure are nothing compared to what others are faced with.

It's interesting how most of us are quick to wish we were in someone else's shoes so we could walk away from our problems. Yet this little exercise proved that most people, when given the chance to trade in their problems for another's, won't, as they realize that everyone has their share of problems and its easier to deal with your own, especially if another's problems make yours look like nothing.

Happiness is not a destination,
it's a method of life.

Unknown

Game Plan

Try this! Before you even attempt to go out and start your day, devise a game plan to help you win before you even begin.

What are we talking about? Every morning when we wake up:

- If we feel depressed, we whistle our favourite tune.
- If we feel angry, we will laugh at ourselves and others.
- If we feel fear, we will face it and move forward.
- If we feel worried, we will take positive action to expel it.
- If we feel incompetent, we will remind ourselves that we have succeeded before.
- If we feel sick, we will think of those far worse off.
- If we feel unsure, we will make sure!
- If we feel inferior, we will raise our heads, stand up straight, push out our chests and stride forward confidently.
- If we feel that we don't matter, we will remember that everyone matters and has something special and unique to offer.

This is our GAME PLAN. What is yours? If you don't have one, why not adopt ours from this moment?

Part 4

Make The Most Of Your Time

'IF ONLY'

An old man lies crying for a life that has been.
A life that seemed but a passing dream.

A lifetime past, so quick, so fast;
Now abruptly ended with the final beat of his heart.

No time even for regrets and 'if only.'
His time has come to find him old and lonely.

Not enough said and not enough done.
Good intentions wasted and no love won.

There's no turning back the hands of Time.
'If only' is something that will never bring him peace of mind.

Sally Eichhorst

Chapter 13

Realise The Value Of Time

If you were going to die soon
and had only one phone call you could make,
who would you call and what would you say?
And why are you waiting?

Stephen Levine

The big birthday bash was to be held the following day. Bill Simmons sat alone in his favourite chair, savouring his last evening at 59 years of age. Tomorrow he would have been on this earth for 60 years. It seemed like a long time, he thought, but in reality it had just flown by. Days became weeks and weeks became months. Then before he knew it the months had multiplied to become the years of his life.

A year ago, Bill had taken early retirement, mainly because of the cancer. He'd been diagnosed as having advanced prostate cancer and had been undergoing treatment for the past year.

After the initial shock of the diagnosis, something happened to Bill that happens to many people who have been given a death scare. Overnight Bill suddenly gained a new and healthy respect for the value of time. Time - this thing that we all so often take for granted because we cling onto the misconception that we have all the time in the world. Bill suddenly woke up to the reality of his own mortality. Like Bill, most of us tend to forget that we all have a time limit on life and we should respect the value of time by making the most of every second available to us.

Isn't it a strange thing that it had taken a death scare to force Bill to really begin living? Knowing that his days may be numbered, he was a changed man. The major difference being, that every second of every day became a precious gift, not to be wasted.

Bill did not want to leave this world regretting anything and up until his diagnosis, it looked like he was going to do just that. However, after he was diagnosed, he took a long, hard look at his life. He was shocked at how much of his time he'd wasted and how much he still wanted to do.

Bill started to insist on quality time with all the people that mattered to him, especially his family, whom he had so often neglected in the past. The small things that had worried him throughout his life fell away. He had no time to waste on feeble worries. The things he'd feared like criticism and failure became unimportant and no longer stopped him from pursuing his dream of opening his own small restaurant. He'd wasted years just thinking about it instead of doing it. Bill's whole attitude and outlook towards life changed. He was determined to be positive and not waste a second being depressed or angry.

Bill was living everyday as though it may be his last by making the most of it. The good news is Bill is still with us, living a happy and fulfilled life running his successful little restaurant.

Whilst enjoying lunch at Bill's restaurant, we noticed an eye catching picture frame on the wall. It was a quote by Mark Twain which read, **'Twenty years from now you will be more disappointed by the things you didn't do than by the ones you did. So throw off the bowlines. Sail away from the safe harbour. Catch the trade winds in your sails.'** Bill later told us that these words helped him to focus on the value of each day and they were up there as a reminder of how short and valuable life really is.

Here is a man who has decided to take every precious day that is given to him and live it to the full. Why don't you do the same?

Dream as if you'll live forever.
Live as if you'll die today.

James Dean

Cherish each second!

Surely you don't want to become like the millions of people all over the world who get to the end of their lives and look back over their time here and realise how they have wasted their lives. If these people could have their lives over again, do you think they would now cherish and make the most of every precious second? You bet they would!

Be honest and ask yourself, 'Do I take risks to grow? Do I love deeply? Do I stand up for myself and my beliefs? Am I striving towards my goals so I can reach my dreams?'

The sad thing is that every day, millions of people die all over the world never reaching their dreams and making the most of their lives. They never took the risks that offered bountiful rewards, never stood up for themselves and their beliefs, never loved for fear of losing it, never reached for their dreams or set goals for fear of criticism or failure, never accomplished much due to procrastination and sheer laziness.

Most people live and die
with their music still unplayed.
They never dare to try.

Mary Kay Ash

What you have to realise is that your time is limited. Everyone, whether they are Presidents, famous celebrities, the richest of men, the poorest of men and **you,** only have 86400 seconds in a day. That's it! No one gets one second more!

Think about this. If you awoke to a new day and were told that this was your last, how would you spend each second of it and how different would it be from your time spent the previous day?

You will probably find that your behaviour, actions, frame of mind, attitude and overall outlook would be totally different. You would certainly want to make the most of every second!

In essence, we should live every day as though it were our last, for we have no way of knowing if indeed it may be. Surely none of us wants to leave this world wishing for so much more from life.

From this moment on, realise the value of your time. Start by thinking back to the last 24 hours! Was this time wasted? What about the next 24 hours? Are you going to waste them as well, or are you going to start making your seconds count?

"Live every day as if it is your last. One day you'll be right."
Anonymous

Chapter 14

Stop Wasting Time!

'Tomorrow is another day...'

Once upon a time there lived a young man.
Procrastination was his name and Life was his game.

He was known to say, 'Tomorrow is another day...'
As he lay around waiting for Opportunity to come his way.

Alas, Opportunity was too late
For Procrastination met with a deadly fate.

Opportunity paid a visit to his grave
And this message he gave,

'I was there all along.
From the moment you were born until the day you died,
I have waited for you', he sighed.

'If you had only looked for me,
You would have found me around every corner, for all to see.'

His gravestone read –
"Procrastination – Today is yours, but alas,
tomorrow is promised to no one."

Sally Eichhorst

'I was away on business the night my Maggie was attacked, ' said Mark. 'I heard the details from the police whilst I held her small, pale hand in mine and looked upon her bruised and battered face. She looked so small, fragile and vulnerable in that hospital bed and I longed for her to open her eyes to see that I was there to protect her from any more harm.

I was informed that burglars had sneaked into our lounge through the sliding doors. The police said they'd obviously broken the latch to gain entry and probably also disarmed the alarm to ensure their entry went unannounced. A flood of guilt welled up inside me as it dawned on me that it was inadvertently my fault. The burglars didn't break the latch and disarm the alarm. I just didn't bother to fix them. I had all the time in the world to fix either the latch or alarm or both, which could have prevented the whole incident or at least warned poor Maggie. I may as well have sent the burglars an open invitation!

I was horrified to hear how the burglars had discovered Maggie and beat her relentlessly, for fun it seems. They left her for dead and made off with everything and anything of any value, which they could carry. Thank goodness a neighbour, returning from an evening out, noticed three suspicious men leaving our home. He called out to them and when they began to run, his suspicions were confirmed and he called the police.

I have always been a procrastinator,' said Mark. 'I guess I just accepted that this was how I was and would always be. I really couldn't see the problem with putting things off for another day. What's the rush anyway? I mean it's not a matter of life or death! Or is it?

This last question haunted me for many days as I sat at

Maggie's bedside. In the end, it was a matter of life and death and all because I procrastinated!

Maggie, my much loved wife and possibly the only thing I'm truly proud of in my life, had been on at me about fixing the latch on our sliding doors. The doors open into our lounge and the latch had been broken for over a month. At first it seemed urgent, as it was a major security risk. I mean anyone could just push the doors open and enter our home without the slightest effort. However, after a few days had passed without anything happening, the urgency fell away and I consoled myself that the fixing of the latch could wait a few more days until I felt like fixing it or having it fixed.

You see, I had the time, although I told myself I didn't. I simply had better things to do or should I say, more pleasurable things to do. The faulty latch wouldn't have posed as much of a security risk if the burglar alarms were working. Of course this was another area of procrastination! Our burglar alarm had gone on the blink several months earlier and became yet another thing I added to my list of things to put off for another day. Something I've now learnt is that 'another day' never comes or comes all too late!

Maggie was unconscious for two weeks, the longest two weeks of my life. I promised myself that if she made it, I would never again put off anything I could and should do today for another day. I would also tell her everyday how much I loved her and needed her. In fact, I would make an effort to spend more time with our family and not endlessly put off get-togethers.

It was during these two weeks that I read your book, 'Unleash your Full Potential.' The section on procrastination really hit home. I realised that procrastination had robbed me of so many opportunities and possibly even my wife. I also realised why I never seemed to get ahead at work or life in general. I was always putting things off! I simply had to stop procrastinating!

The day Maggie awoke, I was afraid she might hate me for inadvertently allowing this to happen to her. I know I hated myself for it! The first words she spoke were, 'I love you' and I am grateful that I have the rest of our lives together to make it up to her and prove myself worthy of her love.

I adopted your phrase, 'Act Now!' to propel me into action when I find myself procrastinating. I felt a little bit silly at first when I sat in front of the TV watching rubbish and repeating the words 'Act Now' to myself. The funny thing is, eventually I couldn't just sit there anymore and had to get up and do something constructive.

I do the same at work now too. If there is something really important I have to do, but it's not a very nice job, I get it done first before I move onto easier and more pleasurable tasks. I've become very good at prioritising and making things happen by just doing what needs to be done instead of continuously putting things off. The end result is that I've recently been promoted from Sales representative to Sales Manager.'

Mark learnt a valuable and life-changing lesson about procrastination. Since he has kicked this habit, (yes, it's simply a bad habit) it has had a profoundly positive affect on all areas of his life. No one is born a procrastinator and must stay one forever. Life is about choices. You can choose to stop procrastinating!

Tomorrow is often the busiest day of the week.

Unknown

So take a moment to think about your life. Are you a procrastinator? If you are, you must get rid of this 'bad habit' or else you will never even come close to achieving any of your goals in life.

A man who has conquered procrastination will never let regrets start taking the place of his dreams

Warren & Sally

The difference between a rut and a grave is their dimensions.

Procrastinators are also experts at getting bogged down in a rut or comfort zone, which is easy and tolerable to begin with, but rapidly becomes depressing and frustrating, stealing months and even years of their lives.

These people are unhappy and complain endlessly about their lives. They keep telling themselves they really must do something about their situation, but they never seem to get around to it. They never seem to find the time in their set routines to make changes for the better. Sure, they can console themselves by saying, 'It's bearable for now,' but in another ten or fifteen years time when nothing has changed and they feel even more stuck in their unhappy situation, it's not so bearable any more.

The only way to break free of a rut is through change. Whether it means a new business venture, a change in a relationship, studying further or travelling, you must force some sort of change so you can grow and better yourself and your situation. **Muhammad Ali explained it so well when he said, "The man who views the world at 50 the same as he did at 20 has wasted 30 years of his life."**

The problem is that we unconsciously seem to become slaves to routine, whether at work or in our relationships. We start to do the same things in the same old ways, day in and day out. Remember that classic saying, ' A Change is as good as a holiday!' Well, try it sometime, it's really refreshing! Life is all about change, learning and growing!

A wise man takes action to change an unhappy situation
The fool does nothing and his life is one continual unhappy situation.
Warren & Sally

Chapter 15

Focus Your Thoughts On The Present

Tomorrow is the most important thing in life . . . comes into us at midnight very clean. It's perfect when it arrives and puts itself in our hands. It hopes we've learned something from yesterday.

John Wayne

Close the door on the dead and distant past

Tina worked as a receptionist for one of our clients and we would often engage her in conversation on our arrival. Eventually, we could accurately predict exactly what she would talk about on every occasion.

All she spoke about was her past, as though the present and future did not exist and her life was already over. She had been divorced for over 10 years and spoke constantly of her failed marriage and how it had ruined her life. She would then fish out her old wedding photo to show us how beautiful she had been and what a wonderful couple her and her husband had made.

Then, the conversation would always steer to how much easier her life had been then and how much happier she was then. She would reminisce over and over about the good old days when things were cheaper, people were friendlier and she was younger and more attractive.

Poor Tina never once spoke to us of what she was going to do today or her plans for tomorrow. For her, there seemed to be no today or tomorrow, only yesterdays.

Tina was retrenched a year ago and just before she left the company, we happened to chat to her once more. Nothing had changed. Her conversation again dwelled on the past and believe it or not, out came the old wedding photo.

Tina's main problem is that her thoughts are dominated by her past. This results in her neglecting the present and therefore not progressing and learning from life.

When your thoughts are always on past victories, previous relationships, opportunities missed and mistakes made, you create within yourself feelings of insecurity, worry, fear and uncertainty, which adversely affect your future decisions.

Don't misunderstand us, it's normal and good to keep happy memories of the past alive, as long as you are intent on making more happy memories instead of hankering only after old ones.

The past can be beneficial only if we use our good memories to motivate us for the future and if we learn from our past mistakes and then put them behind us.

Worrying about the past, wishing for the past, depressing yourself over the events of the past and blaming the past for your present situation is a total waste of your precious time and ultimately gets you nowhere.

"To excel forward in a relationship, a situation,
And most importantly life, One must first forget about the past."
Regina Mckay

There are millions of people like Tina, whose thoughts are dominated by their past. They have no burning desire for a better future, no major goals in life, no drive to better themselves and grow. All they do is exist from day to day with no direction or purpose in life.

The past is dead and gone. It is pointless for anyone to dwell on what was or could have been. To move forward and progress in life, we have to let go of the past. It is impossible to make something worthwhile of our future if we're living in the past. We cannot do anything about the past, but we can do something about today and tomorrow.

When one door closes, another opens. But we often look so regretfully upon the closed door that we don't see the one that has opened for us.
Alexander Graham Bell

Don't miss the magic of the moment by focusing on what's to come.

A wise and ancient soul rocks gently in his chair. Head bowed and heart heavy, he speaks to the wide-eyed little boy before him.

'Don't be like me sonny. Don't miss the magic of the moment! I remember when I was a little lad like you, I couldn't wait to be all grown up. You see, I thought that things would get better as I got older. No more school. No more people telling me what to do and what not to do.

Suddenly, in a flash it seems, I was all grown up and then I couldn't wait to find that perfect job so I could be happy and earn enough money to be content. I found myself wishing it was the weekend already and wishing I was on holiday again. It seemed that when I wasn't wishing for weekends and holidays, I was constantly dreaming of and wishing for better things to come.

Eventually I was wishing for the day that I could retire and put my feet up. I thought surely then I would be happier and things would be a great deal better.'

A cold shiver ran through the old man as he looked at the boy and said, 'One day I woke up and I realised that I had somehow missed the point of it all. I missed out on so much that life had to offer because I was always waiting for and dreaming of better things to come. I forgot that my life wasn't a dress rehearsal, it was the real thing. I always put things off for a special occasion, but I only learnt later that life itself is a special occasion. I constantly wished my life away waiting for a better tomorrow.

I learnt too late that I had put off happiness, fun, love, feeling great about myself and ultimately living. I discovered too late that life is in the living, the capturing of every magical moment.'

The old man leaned over, gently placing his weathered old

hand on the boy's shoulder and said, 'Take it from a wise old man sonny, the best advice I can leave you with is this: don't miss the magic of the moment by focusing on what's to come.'

"Put off living whilst waiting for a better life
and you may wait a lifetime!"

Warren & Sally

There are so many of us who are in the bad habit of putting off living today for a better tomorrow. By all means, dream of good things to come, but you must enjoy the ride along the way. Don't wait for an age, a stage in your life or a dream to come true to really live – live now and enjoy the moment, this hour and every day of your life.

When I win…

There are millions of people waiting for the day to come that they win some major competition or jackpot, in order to have the money they want, to do what they want and live the lives they want. Only then will they allow themselves to be happy.

These people plan their lives around an event, which may never happen. They are headed for disappointment as the day might never arrive, whilst their lives may have wasted away in the meantime.

Isn't it amazing that so many people have this 'When I win… ' psychology? Do you?

Heal and learn from the past, dream and plan for the future, but above all else, **live the present!**

"Yesterday is but a dream, and tomorrow is only a vision, but today well lived makes every yesterday a dream of happiness and every tomorrow a vision of hope."

Unknown

People in general can be grouped into three categories: –

- Those whose thoughts are dominated by their past and are known to say things like, 'This is what I did. This is what I was. This is where I've been.'

- Those whose thoughts are dominated by their distant future and are known to say things like, 'I wish I had.... I wish I were... I wish it was...'

- And those whose thoughts are dominated by the present and are known to say things like, ' This is what I'm going to do. This is what I'm going to be. This is where I'm going.'

So which category do you fall into? Do you find that you are always dwelling on the dead and distant past or focusing on what's to come? Or are you one of the few who have learnt and profited from your past as you stride confidently into the challenging future by making the most of today?

Regardless of which category you fall into, what you must remember is that today will never dawn again. Today is a precious gift that can slip away with alarming speed. Wasted, it will eat a chunk out of your life, but lived well, it will fulfil your life and make it whole.

You cannot live in the past and expect the future to take care of itself. To succeed in life you must live for today and invest in tomorrow.

"It's not the burdens of everyday that drive men mad.
It is the regret of yesterday and the fear of tomorrow.
Regret and fear are twin thieves that rob us of today."

Unknown

Chapter 16

Get The Balance Right!

"The most important leg of a three legged stool is the one that's missing."

Lyall's Fundamental Observation:

We believe that just as a three-legged stool would become unbalanced and fall over if one leg were missing, our lives can fall apart if they are unbalanced. It is our belief that a balanced life is a happy and stable one. A balance between work, family, friends, hobbies, spirituality and any other facet of your life that is important to you, is vital. Concentrating too much on any one area inevitably leads to neglect in others.

Working longer and harder doesn't necessarily make you more effective. If you are neglecting other vital areas of your life, this may eventually actually hamper your effectiveness at work. In the same respect, too much leisure and too little work will also have obvious negative consequences. You have to aim for a balance by planning your day properly.

"Either you run the day or the day runs you."

Jim Rohn

Ask yourself this, 'When I die one day, what will I want people to say about me or remember me for?' Look at any obituary and you will see that no one is remembered for how long and hard they worked or what kind of car they drove and house they lived in. People are remembered for their achievements, being a good parent, good husband, wife or grandparent. They are noted for their kindness, popularity, generosity and humour.

These are the things that really count at the end of the day and yet these are the things so often neglected whilst people strive for success. A truly successful person is a balanced person. Remember there is only so much you can do about the length of your life, but there is a great deal you can do about its width and depth.

"And in the end it's not the years in your life that count.
It's the life in your years."

Abraham Lincoln

Make Time, Not Excuses!

Logan Pearsall Smith said –"There are two things to aim at in life, first, to get what you want; and, after that, to enjoy it. Only the wisest of mankind achieve the second.'

Why is this so? Because there are so many people who concentrate their entire efforts into one area and in the process neglect everything else around them. Their priorities have somehow been lost along the way.

Time is so precious to all of us. In order to get the full benefit of it you must have a balance. In other words, you must make time for that which is important to you.

It's great to put your heart into your work but it's not great if those around you suffer because of it.

You will never find time for anything.
If you want time you must make it.
Charles Buxton

We feel that the following story explains the value of leading a balanced life.

Rick arrived home late from work as usual, both tired and irritable. At the front door waiting for him with the biggest smile you could imagine, was his 6 year old son, Jamey. Before his son could even greet him his father said, ' Not now Jamey, I'm tired. I had a hard day at work so off to bed you go.'

'Okay Daddy,' Jamey replied in a hurt, soft voice. 'But Daddy can I just ask you one question?'

Rick sighed impatiently, 'Okay, but make it quick.'

'Daddy, how much do you earn in one hour at work?' Jamey asked.

'Well son, I earn twenty pounds an hour. Now hurry off to bed, you're blocking the doorway.'

'Sure Daddy, but could I have two pounds please?'

Rick gave his son two pounds and with head down, Jamey shuffled off to his bedroom. Rick then made his way to the kitchen where his wife was busy warming up his dinner. 'You know, you never ever spend time with your son,' his wife blurted out. ' Jamey has been waiting over three hours at the front door for you to come home. Every car that drove past, he thought it was you and started jumping up and down shouting, "Daddy's home". You treat him like this every night. You really must try and make time for him,' she said.

'You know how busy I've been at work Honey,' Rick replied. 'By the time I get home, I'm so tired and all I need is some peace and quiet.'

But Rick did feel a little bit guilty and decided to go upstairs and tuck Jamey in. He opened Jamey's bedroom door and proceeded to sit on the edge of his little bed. Jamey was already asleep, clutching his tattered old teddy bear, Bruno. As Jamey rolled over, Rick caught a glimpse of the two pounds he had given Jamey plus some more money under his pillow. He counted it and arrived at a grand total of eighteen pounds.

Now he was angry. Jamey wanted two pounds of his hard earned money and he already had sixteen pounds. What was the meaning of this?

He woke Jamey up and asked sternly, 'Son, what is all this money under your pillow for? Why did you ask me for money when you clearly had plenty?'

Jamey looked up at his father with his big, sad blue eyes and replied shyly, 'I'm saving up for twenty pounds Daddy, so I can give it to you, so that I can pay you for an hour of your time.'

"It's good to have money and the things that money can buy, but it's good, too, to check once in a while and make sure that you haven't lost things that money can't buy."

Unknown

Part 5

Dare To Reach Your Dreams

" If you can dream it you can do it."
Walt Disney

Chapter 17

Reach For Your Dreams!

" We have learnt that the only failure in life is to never dream and to never try hard enough to reach your dreams."

Sally & Warren

Most of us have many dreams and wishes about what we would like to be or have in life. But for most of us, these remain only dreams and wishes, never to be fulfilled.

Why do so many of us never reach our dreams?

- **Firstly**, most people never quite know what they want from life. Unless you have a crystal-clear idea of what you want from life, there is no way you will accomplish your dreams.

- **Secondly**, if people do know what they want from life, they are often too lazy or feel incapable of taking action to make it happen. Unless you make the effort and take the necessary action to accomplish your dreams, they will never become more than just dreams.

- **Thirdly**, if people do know what they want from life and take action to achieve it, they then lack the perseverance needed to eventually reach their dreams. They attempt one thing and at the first sign of an obstacle, they give up or drop it for another.

In order to live the life of your dreams you must:

- Dare to dream!
- Dare to take action!
- Dare to persevere!

In a nutshell: Dare to reach your dreams.

Let us show you in more detail using 3 simple steps, how you can DARE TO REACH YOUR DREAMS…

Chapter 18

Dare To Dream!

Life is a state of mind,
imagine the one you want,
then create it.

Anonymous

It is our sincere belief that ninety nine percent of people are disillusioned with their lives because they have no clear idea in their minds of what they really want from life.

If you do not have a clear idea of what you want from life, how can you ever hope to achieve anything? In order to live the life of your dreams you must first have a distinct picture of exactly what you want. Knowing what you want is the first step to achieving it.

All great achievers started with a dream and did not question 'how' or 'if' they would achieve it. You must do the same! So dare to dream of all the things you want from life and dare to believe that you can achieve them. Forget 'how' or 'if' - that comes later.

One of the most important things to remember is that there are no limitations to what you want except those that you set for yourself. So do not limit your life by not allowing yourself to imagine great possibilities, for fear that you may not be capable of achieving them.

The human mind has produced wonders such as the possibility of space travel and numerous other once unbelievable and laughable innovations. When we look at technology today, it is obvious that our minds are capable of accomplishing almost anything. So keep your mind open to all possibilities.

As long as you're going to be thinking anyway,
THINK BIG.

Donald Trump

What do you really want?

DO YOU KNOW WHAT YOU REALLY WANT? If not, we strongly recommend that you sit down right now and give this question some serious thought. We cannot over emphasize just how important this is.

Remember, that knowing what you want is the first step to achieving it.

So decide what you really want, no matter how long it takes you and then write it down. Read it every day as often as possible. Only then will you have a crystal clear idea of what you truly want from life. Knowing what you want gives you direction and focus so that at the start of each day you know exactly where you are headed.

If you are unsure about what you really want from life, we recommend that you do the following short exercise.
Imagine that you are ninety years old. You are happily looking

back over your life. What would you like to have seen? What would you have accomplished? Where would you have travelled? What would you have to show for all your years?

Answering these questions should give you a clearer idea of exactly what you want from life.

Chapter 19

Dare To Take Action!

"I must do something" will always solve more problems than "Something must be done."

Anonymous

Why do some people make a success of their lives, attaining all that they dream of, whilst others never achieve much? Do these successful people have some remarkable gift? Are they better looking, more intelligent, from a wealthier background or are they simply luckier than the rest?

Believe it or not, the vast majority of people who have made a success of their lives are no different from you and I. What distinguishes them from those that never achieve much is simply this: they take action to make their dreams a reality.

Begin somewhere.
You cannot build a reputation on what you intend to do.

Liz Smith

If all we needed were dreams to attain our goals, we would all be living our ultimate lives now. Acting on our dreams is what yields results and without positive action, they will remain forever in our imaginations. Don't get us wrong, it's wonderful to dream, but it's only wishful thinking if you're not doing anything to make it happen.

You cannot plough a field by turning it over in your mind.
Anonymous

The problem with taking action is that most people feel it is too difficult or foreboding a task. Before they've even begun, they just give up, not even trying to do anything to make their dreams a reality.

Yes, it's true that there may be so much to do before you reach your goals and often you feel overwhelmed by the enormity of it all, wondering where to even begin.

This is why we believe that the only possible solution to achieving what you want is to do something every day, no matter how small, to move you closer to your goals. When you have big dreams they seem unattainable because they are so far away, but if you keep chipping away at them on a daily basis, before you know it you will have achieved them. Whilst chipping away at your goals remember this famous saying by Lao-tzu, **'A journey of a thousand miles must begin with a single step.'** So begin your journey now!

Don't wait for your ship to come in...
Swim out and get it.

Unknown

Pick the bone that best describes you:

Wishbone – a wishful thinker, who dreams, but never acts. Wishes and waits for others to do the work or for things to fall into his or her lap.

Jawbone – a big talker, with little or no action to follow. Excellent at whinging and whining, but not good at doing anything about it.

Knucklebone – stands back and knocks everything anyone else does or tries. Excellent at criticising although he or she won't try themselves. Even better at blaming people or other things for his or her lack of success and failures.

Backbone – the one who takes responsibility for the load. This is the one who does the work, takes action and makes things happen. Without this person everything collapses and comes to a grinding halt. Nothing can move forward or grow without the backbone!

Even if you are on the right track,
you'll get run over if you just sit there.

Will Rogers

If you have a crystal clear idea of what you want, you have to ask yourself this one important question: 'What am I doing to get there?' Most who have led successful lives are doers. They chose to take action and so can you!

Chapter 20

Dare To Persevere!

Perseverance is the bridge between goals and accomplishment.
Warren & Sally

There was an experiment conducted several years ago on a group of pre-schoolers. They were told that they could either have one marshmallow right now, or if they waited for an hour, they could have five marshmallows.

What do you think happened? Almost all the kids opted for one marshmallow right now and only a handful were willing to wait an hour to receive the prize of five marshmallows. This small handful had already learnt from an early age about concentrating on the big picture. They were willing to sacrifice a short-term fix for a larger reward in the long-term. So what? Well, a longitudinal study was performed on all these pre-schoolers and it was found that the small percentage who had learnt this early lesson were a lot more successful in their later years than the others.

These children realised the value of holding out for 100% later, rather than only 2% now and carried this lesson with them through life. They therefore achieved most of their goals as they could persevere to reach their goals rather than allowing themselves to be tempted or side-tracked by short-term benefits or instant gratification.

The way I see it,
if you want the rainbow,
you gotta be willing to put up with the rain.
Dolly Parton

It's wonderful if you are taking action to get what you want from life. But it is no good if you give up at the first obstacle that comes your way. You must learn to persevere! Remember that failure is merely a detour on the road to success .

Perseverance should not be confused with 'hard work' or 'the number of hours worked'. It can be more accurately defined as your total commitment and determination to follow through with your plan, even in the face of defeat and criticism. It is knowing what you want and being so determined to have it that you commit your entire efforts to getting it. It means having the willpower to fight on when others wave the flag of defeat. It is the quality that truly separates the winners from the losers.

To succeed in anything, you must learn to develop perseverance, or else you will fail, no matter how worthy your goal.

Obstacles don't have to stop you.
If you run into a wall, don't turn around and give up.
Figure out how to climb it, go through it, or work around it.
Michael Jordan

Is it worth it?

The question is, how do you develop perseverance? Quite simply, what you are striving for must be worth it to you! Remember that if you have enough reasons to do something, you will be far more motivated to do it. It must be worth the time, effort and resources you must sacrifice to achieve it.

Perseverance makes all the difference between failing and winning! Without perseverance you have lost before you have even begun. No matter how often you fall and are knocked back down again and again, you are never a failure if you keep picking yourself up to try again. The only failure is in giving up and staying down. Remember, the spirit of the true champion is found in those who pick themselves up every time to try again. When you have perseverance you will win even when the deck is stacked against you.

Our greatest glory is not in never failing,
but in rising up every time we fail.
Ralph Waldo Emerson

It took Alex Haley 17 years to achieve his goal! He left a 20 year career in the Coast Guard to realise his dream of becoming a writer. When things went wrong he often felt he should just give up but his perseverance kept him going.

17 years after leaving the Coast Guard, he became the best selling author of 'Roots', which won 9 Emmy awards and was made into a T.V. mini-series.

This is the type of persistence few have, but those that do

possess it always achieve their ultimate dreams. They realise that the toughest part of getting to the top of the ladder, is getting through the crowd at the bottom.

Without perseverance you will not win and the rewards you dreamed of will always remain out of your grasp; a mere figment of your imagination. Next to knowing what you want, perseverance is probably the single most important quality, anyone who is interested in succeeding, could ever possess. Develop this quality and it will carry you when you are down, lifting you and urging you to push on until you reach your dreams.

" It does not matter how slowly you go
as long as you do not stop."

Confucius

Ever wondered how dolphin trainers get their dolphins to jump a couple of metres out of the water and perform tricks? To train them is obviously a great challenge, which is similar to the challenges we must face if we are to achieve what we want in life.

So how would the average person approach the problem of training dolphins to jump out of the water and over a rope? They know what they want. They want the dolphins to jump over a rope held 2 metres above the water. So they raise a rope 2 metres above the water and stand up there, dangling some fish as a reward, expectantly waiting for the dolphins to do their thing. Do they jump over the rope? We don't think so! So what does the average person then do? Eventually they give up.

That is exactly how many people try to achieve what they want. They know what they want. Maybe they want to look good. So what do they do? They join the gym expecting to see results immediately. Failing to achieve this, they give up, ready to try again only when they can't bear to see themselves in the mirror anymore. Maybe they want to earn good money. They want the good life; the expensive cars; the lovely clothes; the house on the beach and being their own boss. But how much effort do they put in to make it all happen? In most cases they give up as soon as things look too difficult or obstacles come their way.

Effort only releases its reward after a person refuses to quit.
Napoleon Hill

Here is what they should be doing.....

Let's go back to dolphin training. So how do they train the dolphins to jump over the rope?

Well, first they put the rope under the water so that the dolphin just cannot help but go over the rope. Every time they go over the rope, they get fish and they get played with. Most importantly however, they get the belief that they can do it.

But what happens if one or more of the dolphins goes under the rope? Nothing! Dolphins are taught that the negative behaviour must be ignored. The trainer slowly raises the rope making sure that the dolphins can always clear it. Eventually it is raised to 2 metres above the water and the dolphins clear it easily. They do eventually reach their goal!

Would this work for us? You bet!

You are halfway to achieving your goal when you know what you want and you progress towards it, ignoring all the negatives along the way. You will definitely reach your ultimate goal, if you move closer towards it everyday, no matter how small the movement. Eventually through trial, error and effort, it will be yours.

There is but one secret to success -
NEVER GIVE UP!

Unknown

Winners versus Losers

The Winner is always a part of the answer;
The Loser is always a part of the problem.
The Winner always has a programme;
The Loser always has an excuse.
The Winner says, "Let me do it for you;"
The Loser says, "That's not my job."
The Winner sees an answer for every problem;
The Loser sees a problem in every answer.
The Winner says,
"It may be difficult but it's possible;"
The Loser says,
"It may be possible but it's too difficult."

Unknown

" As long as I'm faced in the right direction,
It does not matter the size of my steps."

Unknown

Conclusion

" It's not where you start that matters, but where you finish."

Unknown

With the research for our books, the experiences others have shared with us, trial and error and especially what we have come to understand along the way, we have arrived at the following conclusions....

- We've concluded that it's not what you have in life, but who you have and who you are in life that counts.
- We've concluded that you should never compare yourself to the best others can do, but rather to the best you can do.
- We've concluded that it is not what happens to us that's important. It's what we do about it.
- We've concluded that we should all think before we react.
- We've concluded that we can all keep going long after we believe we can't.
- We've concluded that no matter what the situation, there are always two sides to the story.
- We've concluded that becoming the people we want to be is a constant process.
- We've concluded that we are responsible for our own actions, choices and decisions, no matter what.

- We've concluded that we must control our attitude or else it will control us.

- We've concluded that true champions are those who take action when it is needed, to do what is required and accept responsibility, regardless of the consequences.

- We've concluded that learning to forgive and/or forget takes practice.

- We've concluded that maturity is not age related. It's more a matter of what types of experiences you've had and the lessons you've learnt from them.

- We've concluded that we should never tell anyone that their dreams are impossible or far-fetched, especially ourselves because people without dreams don't have much.

- We've concluded that who we are may have been influenced by our background and circumstances, but at the end of the day, we are all responsible for who we choose to become.

- We've concluded that life has a great deal to do with perception or interpretation. Several people can look at exactly the same thing and they may all see something completely different.

- We've concluded that the mind of man is more powerful than we could ever imagine and the trick to tapping into this power is self-control.

- We've concluded that money, material assets, power, fame, knowledge, intelligence and credentials on the wall do not necessarily make you a decent human being.

- We've concluded that you should give people more than they expect and do it cheerfully.

- We've concluded that when you say, "I love you," or "I'm sorry," you should mean it.

- We've concluded that you should love deeply and passionately although you risk getting hurt, as it's the only way to live life completely.

- We've concluded that great love and great achievements involve great risks but are well worth it.

- We've concluded that you should not judge others by their relatives or the life they happened to be born into.

- We've concluded that you never lose unless you lose the lesson.

- We've concluded that you should not let a little dispute injure a great friendship.

- We've concluded that you should read more books, keeping in mind that television is no substitute.

- We've concluded that you should do all you can to create a tranquil, harmonious and stress free home and environment for yourself.

- We've concluded that in disagreements with loved ones, you should deal only with the current situation and forget the past.

- We've concluded that you should not just listen to what someone is saying but also to why they are saying it.

- We've concluded that if you make a lot of money, put it to use helping others while you are living. It is truly wealth's greatest satisfaction.

- We've concluded that you should always judge your success by what you had to give up or sacrifice in order to get it.

- We've concluded that life's too short to leave things for another day, as we may not have another day.

- We've concluded that you should always DO THE RIGHT THING - so when it comes time for you to think back, you'll be able to enjoy it a second time rather than regret it for a lifetime.

It's a funny thing…

It's a funny thing - this time we live in. A time of wide and complicated highways, but narrow and simple viewpoints. A time of increased spending, but less to show for it.

What about all the conveniences to save time, yet we have less time? There are also plenty of experts, but more problems. There are so many more medical options, yet less wellness.

We watch our possessions grow whilst our values shrink. We know how to make a living, but have forgotten how to make a life. We seem to buy so much more and yet enjoy it so much less. Our incomes may have grown, but our morals have shrunk. It's a time of quantity rather than quality.

Above all this however, it's a time when you can choose to do what it takes to make a difference for the better.

Whether it means simply keeping an open mind or building strong, respectable values and morals or making the most of your life and enjoying it to the full.

It is definitely a time of greater opportunities and an abundance of choices for you to make the most of.

It is indeed a time when your success can only depend on you!

Any correspondence or enquiries to be addressed to :

Reach Publishers & Workshops
P.O.Box 1384
Wandsbeck
South Africa
3631